CliffsNotes™

Morrison's

Beloved

**By Mary Robinson, M.A.
and Kris Fulkerson, M.A.**

IN THIS BOOK

- Learn about the life and writings of Toni Morrison
- Preview an introduction to *Beloved*
- Explore the novel's themes and character development in the Critical Commentaries
- Examine in-depth Character Analyses
- Acquire an understanding of key themes with Critical Essays
- Reinforce what you learn with CliffsNotes Review
- Find additional information to further your study in CliffsNotes Resource Center and online at www.cliffsnotes.com

IDG Books Worldwide, Inc.
An International Data Group Company
Foster City, CA • Chicago, IL • Indianapolis, IN • New York, NY

Publisher's Acknowledgments
Editorial
    Project Editor: Joan Friedman
    Acquisitions Editor: Gregory W. Tubach
    Copy Editor: Billie A. Williams
    Glossary Editors: The editors and staff at Webster's
    New World™ Dictionaries
    Editorial Administrator: Michelle Hacker

Production
    Indexer: York Production Services, Inc.
    Proofreader: York Production Services, Inc.
    IDG Books Indianapolis Production Department

CliffsNotes™ Morrison's *Beloved*
Published by
IDG Books Worldwide, Inc.
An International Data Group Company
919 E. Hillsdale Blvd.
Suite 300
Foster City, CA 94404

www.idgbooks.com (IDG Books Worldwide Web site)
www.cliffsnotes.com (CliffsNotes Web site)

Library of Congress Control Number: 00-108204

ISBN: 0-7645-8667-X

Printed in the United States of America

10 9 8 7 6 5 4 3 2 1

1O/RT/RR/QQ/IN

Distributed in the United States by IDG Books Worldwide, Inc.

Distributed by CDG Books Canada Inc. for Canada; by Transworld Publishers Limited in the United Kingdom; by IDG Norge Books for Norway; by IDG Sweden Books for Sweden; by IDG Books Australia Publishing Corporation Pty. Ltd. for Australia and New Zealand; by TransQuest Publishers Pte Ltd. for Singapore, Malaysia, Thailand, Indonesia, and Hong Kong; by Gotop Information Inc. for Taiwan; by ICG Muse, Inc. for Japan; by Norma Comunicaciones S.A. for Columbia; by Intersoft for South Africa; by Eyrolles for France; by International Thomson Publishing for Germany, Austria and Switzerland; by Distribuidora Cuspide for Argentina; by LR International for Brazil; by Galileo Libros for Chile; by Ediciones ZETA S.C.R. Ltda. for Peru; by WS Computer Publishing Corporation, Inc., for the Philippines; by Contemporanea de Ediciones for Venezuela; by Express Computer Distributors for the Caribbean and West Indies; by Micronesia Media Distributor, Inc. for Micronesia; by Grupo Editorial Norma S.A. for Guatemala; by Chips Computadoras S.A. de C.V. for Mexico; by Editorial Norma de Panama S.A. for Panama; by American Bookshops for Finland. Authorized Sales Agent: Anthony Rudkin Associates for the Middle East and North Africa.

For general information on IDG Books Worldwide's books in the U.S., please call our Consumer Customer Service department at **800-762-2974**. For reseller information, including discounts and premium sales, please call our Reseller Customer Service department at **800-434-3422**.

For information on where to purchase IDG Books Worldwide's books outside the U.S., please contact our International Sales department at **317-572-3993** or fax **317-572-4002**.

For consumer information on foreign language translations, please contact our Customer Service department at **1-800-434-3422**, fax **317-572-4002**, or e-mail rights@idgbooks.com.

For information on licensing foreign or domestic rights, please phone **+1-650-653-7098**.

For sales inquiries and special prices for bulk quantities, please contact our Order Services department at **800-434-3422** or write to the address above.

For information on using IDG Books Worldwide's books in the classroom or for ordering examination copies, please contact our Educational Sales department at **800-434-2086** or fax **317-572-4005**.

For press review copies, author interviews, or other publicity information, please contact our Public Relations department at **650-653-7000** or fax **650-653-7500**.

For authorization to photocopy items for corporate, personal, or educational use, please contact Copyright Clearance Center, 222 Rosewood Drive, Danvers, MA 01923, or fax **978-750-4470**.

Table of Contents

Life and Background of the Author 1
  Personal Background 2
  Teaching and Writing 4
  Critical Response.. 8
  Honors 9

Introduction to the Novel. 11
  Introduction 12
  A Brief Synopsis.. 12
  List of Characters.. 14
  A Brief Chronology of the Events in *Beloved* 17
  Character Map... 21

Critical Commentaries 22
  Epigraph 23
  Chapter 1 24
    Summary... 24
    Commentary.. 25
    Glossary.. 26
  Chapter 2 28
    Summary... 28
    Commentary.. 28
    Glossary.. 29
  Chapter 3 30
    Summary... 30
    Commentary.. 30
    Glossary.. 31
  Chapter 4 33
    Summary... 33
    Commentary.. 33
    Glossary.. 34
  Chapter 5 35
    Summary... 35
    Commentary.. 35
    Glossary.. 36
  Chapter 6 37
    Summary... 37
    Commentary.. 38
    Glossary.. 38
  Chapter 7 39
    Summary... 39
    Commentary.. 40
    Glossary.. 41
  Chapter 8 42
    Summary... 42
    Commentary.. 42
    Glossary.. 44

Chapter 9 45
    Summary 45
    Commentary 46
    Glossary 47
Chapter 10 48
    Summary 48
    Commentary 48
    Glossary 49
Chapter 11 51
    Summary 51
    Commentary 51
    Glossary 52
Chapter 12 53
    Summary 53
    Commentary 53
    Glossary 55
Chapters 13 and 14 56
    Summary 56
    Commentary 57
    Glossary 58
Chapter 15 59
    Summary 59
    Commentary 60
    Glossary 60
Chapter 16 61
    Summary 61
    Commentary 62
    Glossary 62
Chapters 17 and 18 63
    Summary 63
    Commentary 63
    Glossary 65
Chapter 19 66
    Summary 66
    Commentary 67
    Glossary 68
Chapters 20 and 21 71
    Summary 71
    Commentary 71
Chapters 22 and 23 73
    Summary 73
    Commentary 73
Chapter 24 75
    Summary 75
    Commentary 76
    Glossary 77

taught her daughter to avoid animosity. (However, an experience with insect-riddled food from the welfare dole provoked Mrs. Wofford to write a letter of complaint to President Franklin Roosevelt.)

Brought up in a nurturing, religious environment, Morrison says, "We were taught that as individuals we had value, irrespective of what the future might hold for us. The women of the black community, whether aunt, grandmother, or neighbor, served as a tightly woven safety net." The oral tradition, carried on by both men and women, cushioned blows to self-esteem with stories and songs about the Underground Railroad, daring rescues, and other perils and triumphs of black history. In addition, Morrison absorbed stories about the post-Reconstruction South from her maternal grandparents, John Solomon and Ardelia Willis, who emigrated from Alabama in 1912.

Stronger than the men in Morrison's memory, the women of the black community were, as she says, "liberated women of the world, who could shroud the dead, nudge African violets into bloom, make beautiful biscuits, plow; they could hold you in their arms, honey, and you'd think you were in heaven." Morrison felt an obligation to these larger-than-life role models, and she recognized that "whatever I did was easy in comparison with what they had to go through."

Education

A born mimic, actor, storyteller, and reader from early childhood, Morrison was expected to excel, even though she had to fight the paranoia that accompanied growing up in an educational milieu that ignored the contributions of nonwhites. Undeterred, she wrote and told stories, read poetry, and followed the example of ballerina Maria Tallchief, who Morrison idolized for her ability to promote her Native American culture while simultaneously enriching the arts. At Lorain High School, Morrison completed four years of Latin and graduated at the top of her class. She then surprised her family by insisting on leaving Lorain to obtain a college degree, which her father paid for by working three jobs.

Having educated herself in the achievements of blacks, Morrison—already steeped in the fiction of French, English, and Russian novelists—entered Howard University in Washington, D.C., where she changed her first name to Toni. She studied under strong African-American spokesmen: poet Sterling Brown and philosopher and critic Alain Locke, a Rhodes scholar who edited *The New Negro*.

Morrison received the standard English education: a strong grounding in the white males who dominate literature—Shakespeare, Hawthorne, Melville, and Wordsworth. She immersed herself in the Howard Unity Players, the university repertory company, and toured the South for the first time, playing to black audiences during the unsettled pre-civil rights era. Morrison graduated with a B.A. in 1953 and completed a master's degree in English at Cornell two years later, with a concentration in the work of Virginia Woolf and William Faulkner.

Teaching and Writing

The first two years after Cornell, Morrison taught humanities and English at Texas Southern University. She then worked for eight years as an English instructor at Howard University. Her two most promising students were civil rights activist Stokely Carmichael and Claude Brown, author of *Manchild in the Promised Land.* The year after she left teaching, Morrison gravitated toward writing. She joined a monthly literary symposium in 1962 and contributed stories that she had begun in high school. Chief among them was a story she read aloud about a black girl who wanted to make up for her shortcomings by petitioning God for blue eyes.

By that time, Morrison's 1957 marriage to Jamaican architect Harold Morrison had produced a son, Harold Ford, born in 1962. She ended the marriage in 1965, returned to Lorain for a year and a half (during which her second child, Slade Kevin, was born), and renewed her literary outlet as an antidote to loneliness. Explaining her urge to write, she emphasizes a need for "books that I had wanted to read. No one had written them yet, so I wrote them."

From 1965 to 1983, Morrison served as a textbook editor at Random House, working from her home in Syracuse, New York. The move from Ohio alarmed her mother, who admonished, "You don't have anybody there." Self-assured of her ambitions, Morrison replied, "You take the village with you. There is no need for the community if you have a sense of it inside."

Tending to two small sons and a demanding job, she still managed to plug away at *The Bluest Eye,* her personal therapy for depression and isolation. Set in the Midwest, the story centers on a compelling, unloved child, Pecola Breedlove, a victim of incest and a survivor of ego abuse. As Morrison describes the compulsion to complete the manuscript, "I had no will, no judgment, no perspective, no power, no authority, no self—just this brutal sense of irony, melancholy, and a trembling respect for words. I wrote like someone with a dirty habit. Secretly—compulsively—slyly." The novel is a haunting portrayal of a marginal child, one so unlovely, so unloved that she finds no reclamation. As Morrison concludes Pecola's tragic destruction, "[O]n the edge of my town, among the garbage and the sunflowers of my town, it's much, much, much too late."

By the time the manuscript was complete in 1968, Morrison had risen to the rank of senior editor at Random House company headquarters in New York City, where, as developer of black talent, she groomed such stars as Angela Davis, Toni Cade Bambara, Wesley Brown, Gayl Jones, and Muhammad Ali. She reports that her own first novel sold for racial reasons: The company wanted a black writer in its stable. When the black fiction market burgeoned, Morrison reminded herself that the trend reflected the honor accorded the struggles of the black race. To steady herself on such holy ground, she repeated a mantra recalling the "very real life-threatening obstacles people in my family face, and whenever I would feel overwhelmed, that's all I had to think about."

As a senior editor, Morrison became immersed in contemporary literature and was aware of an upsurge in black literary voices. Buoyed by this upsurge, in 1969, she returned to the classroom for a year as the Albert Schweitzer Professor of Humanities at State University of New York in Purchase. She settled into a renovated boathouse outside the town of Nyack and kept writing. Four years later, she completed *Sula,* her second novel, which continues her demarcation of the black woman's world, with its secret power, perversity, unity, and mysticism. The critics were divided on the character's murder of her drug-dealing son, a sign of something sinister and unsettling and an omen of ghetto life in the coming decades. More popular than *The Bluest Eye,* the second novel was excerpted in *Redbook* and featured as a Book-of-the-Month Club alternate.

As Morrison's name began to take on public recognition, her byline appeared more frequently on book reviews for the *New York Times.* In 1974, she compiled a memory album, *The Black Book,* which was introduced by Bill Cosby as a "folk journey of Black America." Composed of oddments from slave narratives, advertising, photographs, media clippings, recipes, and patent office records, the book revealed three centuries of black history in the United States. The research was almost like a remedial cultural education for Morrison—an education that had been denied previously. Her "literary archeology" provided a cache of motifs, themes, and images for later fiction. It also unearthed a clipping from a nineteenth-century magazine that would inspire *Beloved*.

During the next decade, visiting lecturer posts drew Morrison to Yale from 1975–1977 and Bard College from 1979–1980. The need to express beliefs and truths from her active imagination led in 1977 to the publication of *Song of Solomon*, a Midwestern saga strongly influenced by the death of her father. Like a patchwork vision of her collective unconscious, the novel draws on family lore and a wisdom sprung from survival. In Morrison's words, her forebears became "my entrance into my own interior life." *Song of Solomon* is a mythic tale centering on slaves who fly to Africa. The novel's success, a popular television interview with Dick Cavett, and inclusion in the PBS series "Writers in America" brought Toni Morrison to the forefront of American fiction.

Within four years, Morrison followed up on the promise of earlier works with *Tar Baby*. In a provocative departure from her earlier all-black casts, *Tar Baby* introduced the ambivalent Jadine, a world-weary traveler who searches for self-actualization among West Indian servant-caste relatives through a brief fling with a mysterious black man. Critics were divided as to the direction that Morrison seemed to be moving as she departed from less familiar themes, characters, and settings. Nonetheless, Morrison became the first black woman championed in a cover story for *Newsweek,* which heralded her as the top black writer in the United States. Her response was a teasing one-liner: "Are you really going to put a middle-aged, gray-haired, colored lady on the cover of this magazine?"

In January 1986, the New York State Writers Institute commissioned Morrison to write *Dreaming Emmett,* a dramatization of the murder of 14-year-old Emmett Till by Mississippi racists in the 1950s. Having proven herself worthy of stage production from the writing of the musical *Storyville* and a screen version of *Tar Baby,* she felt equal to the task of recreating the grisly murder, which was presented in Albany by the Capital Repertory Company.

Three years after *Dreaming Emmett* was produced, Morrison published her fifth novel, *Beloved.* With this novel, Morrison returned to a focus on women. The novel arose from Morrison's ten-year contemplation of a slave narrative featuring Margaret Garner, a Kentucky slave woman who murdered one of her four children in 1855 rather than submit her family to what Morrison terms "creative cruelty."

Beloved probes the paradox of motherhood within slavery. This paradox is revealed through the humiliation of Sethe (the character inspired by Garner) and her desperate murder of her infant daughter. Intent on honoring an extraordinary act of maternal love, Morrison had incubated the characters for two years and then withdrew into her house and wrote Sethe's story in longhand. Strengthened by research provided by writer Michael Blitz from sources as far away as Brazil and Spain, she salted the powerful narrative with details about labor opportunities for blacks along the Ohio River, housing, clothing, furniture, prices, torture devices to constrain the tongue or keep a slave from sleeping, Cincinnati society, and particularly white abolitionists who were the black population's lifeline after passage of the Fugitive Slave Laws and during Reconstruction.

To keep an artistic perspective on the fictional Sethe, Morrison departed from the story of the real Margaret Garner, who was returned to her owner. Morrison fictionalizes the scene in which the cruel slave-master known only as "schoolteacher" returns to Kentucky without Sethe and her children, but the book's dedication reminds the reader that, at heart, Morrison deals with reality. The "sixty million and more" she refers to in the dedication are the victims of two centuries of slavery, the ones who did not escape drowning, disease, sharks, whipping, mutilation, burning, boiling, rape, emasculation, starvation, and other horrors. Justifying her choice of the highest number of victims that scholars offer, Morrison explained, "I didn't want to leave anybody out."

In 1992, Morrison published *Jazz,* the story of Joe Trace; his wife, Violet; and his lover, Dorcas, whom he murders. The book is set against events in African American history from 1880 through 1926, with much of the main story taking place in Harlem in the 1920s. The novel explores the themes of community, artistic expression, and personal growth, using blues and jazz to represent the importance of change.

Morrison continued her exploration of the black community in 1998's *Paradise.* The novel explores the history of Ruby, Oklahoma, an all-black town where its residents learn that isolating themselves from the rest of the world does not guarantee freedom from oppression or exclusion.

Currently, Morrison devotes a great deal of time to a host of speaking engagements plus honorary memberships in organizations such as the Center for the Study of Southern Culture, New York Public Library, Helsinki Watch Committee, and the advisory council of New York's Queens College.

Critical Response

Reviewers, often more certain of Morrison's success than the author herself, have lauded the quality and power in her brutal yet tender honesty, her melodrama, and her use of oral tradition and myth. Reviewing her first novel, Ruby Dee wrote, "I've just finished reading Toni Morrison's book *The Bluest Eye* and my heart hurts." Marcia Ann Gillespie, former *Ms.* Editor-in-chief, says that "Morrison's women—some are big, powerful people, others shadows and totally powerless, some risk takers, others safety seekers." She adds that "through all of them, Morrison asks us, What's power? What's love? What's the real cost of living? Who and what can you claim and/or control? What tricks do you have to play in order to get through? How do you define yourself?" Such perceptive interrogation reminds us that Morrison questions more than black/white relations; she probes humanistic terrain.

Critic Nellie Y. McKay, a strong supporter of Toni Morrison's approach to fiction, celebrates her imaginative flow and control of inner dialogue. Comparing her skills to those of James Joyce and William Faulkner, McKay notes that Morrison has absorbed the styles and methods of significant literary movements and periods, yet she remains true to her own understanding of what it means to be black—to look through the collective eyes of an entire race. As Toni Cade Bambara says, Morrison is "grand and majestic"; she is a writer who "courageously tackles the big issues all the time. She's not small."

By escaping Eurocentrism—that is, the Caucasian point of view—Morrison has liberated and expanded literature in the same way that Jelly Roll Morton, Thelonious Monk, Cannonball Adderley, John Coltrane, Bessie Smith, Louis Armstrong, Bill Robinson, Josephine Baker, Judith Jamison, and Spike Lee liberated and expanded music, dance, and film. Critic Dan Cryer describes Morrison's novels depicting African-American life as "fluid and lyrical, as full of sorrow and gusto as the blues, at once eloquent laments for her people and tributes to their staying power." The refusal to quit, to knuckle under, or to cower in self-doubt makes her characters memorable and, more important, admirable.

For Morrison, merging into the psyche of the character produces a mystical "something"—an awareness that approaches a séance, an out-of-self experience akin to communing with spirits of a former time and place. Her ability to identify with and actualize fictional creations has earned her the nickname "conjure woman." Her belief that such expression draws on a collective consciousness of music and oral traditions—of stories that exist in a fragile, ephemeral state because they have yet to appear on paper—leads her to think of her art as political. Because she writes from an almost devout concern for the characters who people her imaginary landscapes, Morrison produces a quality of fiction that transcends race, gender, social or political circumstance, and time.

Honors

On a par with Gwendolyn Brooks, Maya Angelou, Mari Evans, Alice Walker, and Toni Cade Bambara, Toni Morrison has proven that African-American women writers no longer command only a black audience but can hold white readers' interest and earn their respect while lessening their ignorance of the black race. With the publication of *Song of Solomon*, Morrison began setting records for achievements, beginning with a National Book Award and the Ohioana Book Award in 1975 and advancing to an appointment to the National Council on the Arts in 1980 by President Jimmy Carter.

The first black female to produce a Book-of-the-Month Club key selection, Morrison won a $3,000 stipend from the American Academy and Institute of Arts and Letters, three consecutive Public Library Books for the Teen Age, and awards from the New York State Governor's Arts Council, City College of New York Langston Hughes Festival, and the Anisfield-Wolf Book Award. As evidence of her substantial presence in the literary world, in 1981 Morrison was invited to address the American Writers' Congress.

In January 1988 (only a few months after James Baldwin died unsung in American literary circles), Morrison was nominated for Ritz-Hemingway, National Book, and National Book Critics Circle awards but won none of them. Led by poet June Jordan, a formal protest ran in major newspapers, accompanied by an open letter from Maya Angelou, Amiri Baraka, Henry Louis Gates, Alice Walker, John Edgar Wideman, Angela Davis, and 42 other black colleagues who decried the slight of Morrison's accomplishment. Morrison's supporters argued that she advances "the moral and artistic standards by which we must measure the daring and love of our national imagination and our collective intelligence as a people." Critic Houston A. Baker labeled the action a "civil action" designed to call attention to a "miscarriage of judgment." He explained, "We wanted to call the attention of others to this ignoring of the beauty and greatness of Morrison. This is egregious."

Morrison was stunned by the support of her peers. On March 31, 1988, she won a Pulitzer Prize for *Beloved,* which had enjoyed an 18-week run on the bestseller list. That same cataclysmic year, a list of awards came tumbling after: the Melcher Book Award, Robert F. Kennedy Book Award, Peggy V. Helmerich Distinguished Author Award, and the City of New York Mayor's Award of Honor for Art and Culture. From New York University came the Elmer Holmes Bobst Award in Arts and Letters, marked by a medal and $2,000. Fourteen honorary degrees poured in from mostly east coast institutions, notably Oberlin, Dartmouth, Bryn Mawr, Columbia, and Yale. Morrison was named Tanner Lecturer at the University of Michigan.

The literary matriarch accepted her windfall, winning audiences with soft-spoken grace and a private, understated sense of self. "It was fabulous," she said. "I loved it. I felt crowned."

In fall 1989, Morrison left her Albany home to accept the Robert Goheen Professorship in creative writing, women's studies, and African studies at Princeton, becoming the first black female to be so honored by the Ivy League. That same year she received the MLA Commonwealth Award, and the following year brought the Chianti Ruffino Antico Fattore International Literary Prize.

In 1993, Morrison became the first black woman to win the Nobel Prize for literature. The Nobel Foundation stated that Morrison "gives life to an essential aspect of American reality" through "novels characterized by visionary force and poetic import."

INTRODUCTION TO THE NOVEL

Introduction. 12

A Brief Synopsis 12

List of Characters 14

A Brief Chronology of the Events
in *Beloved* 17

Character Map 21

Introduction

Beloved, which is classified as historical fiction, gothic horror story, and *bildungsroman* (coming-of-age novel), demonstrates Toni Morrison's skill in penetrating the unconstrained, unapologetic psyches of numerous characters who shoulder the horrific burden of slavery's hidden sins. Because the crimes at the heart of the novel repulse some readers, a small vocal coterie of critics has lambasted Morrison's work as soap opera, a "blackface holocaust novel," and a revamped *Heart of Darkness.* In rebuttal, she has insisted, "It's not my job to make black peoples' values acceptable to society as a whole." Rather, Morrison chooses to marvel that slaves who were brutalized beyond endurance were able to function as well as they did, especially after emancipation, when their expectations were high but their social station reflected little change from plantation days.

Morrison drew on a Cincinnati murder case arising from a woman's sacrifice of her children to keep them out of the grasp of slave catchers. As Morrison saw it, slavery denied black mothers the right to feel maternal love and eventually made them ambivalent toward their own offspring, particularly those sired by slave ship crews, overseers, and masters. In her words, "[These women] were not mothers but breeders." In *Beloved,* Morrison explores the psychology of motherhood when a slave mother and her children experience freedom. No longer a "breeder," the mother is free to love her children absolutely and, therefore, becomes capable of making unthinkable sacrifices to protect them.

The power of *Beloved* lies in Morrison's ability to create a compelling curiosity about the nature of Sethe's crime. Less a suspense novel than a treatise on acceptance and endurance, the work has struck an appreciative chord with a varied audience, including many noted authors who value the painful process of creating a guilt-ridden, near-crazed survivor. By identifying with the piercing eye and halting voice of a child-killer, Morrison performs what critic Claudia Tate calls "reclamation of slavery" through empathy with Sethe's will to endure and to love on her own terms.

A Brief Synopsis

Beloved is not narrated chronologically; it is composed of flashbacks, memories, and nightmares. As a result, it is not an easy read if you haven't encountered William Faulkner, James Joyce, or Virginia Woolf. Following, we have constructed a basic outline of the action in the story. In no way, however, does it reflect the wonder of Morrison's novel.

Sethe, a 13-year-old child of unnamed slave parents, arrives at Sweet Home, an idyllic plantation in Kentucky operated by Garner, an unusually humane master, and his wife, Lillian. Within a year, Sethe selects Halle Suggs to be her mate and, by the time she is 18, bears him three children. After Garner dies, his wife turns control of the plantation over to her brother-in-law, the schoolteacher, who proves to be a brutal overseer.

Schoolteacher's cruelty drives the Sweet Home slave men—Paul D, Halle, Paul A, and Sixo—to plot their escape. In August, fearful that her sons will be sold, a very pregnant Sethe packs her children Howard, Buglar, and Beloved in a wagon and sends them to safety with their grandmother in Cincinnati. Schoolteacher discovers what she has done, and as Halle watches from the loft of a barn, schoolteacher takes notes as his nephews—the "two boys with mossy teeth"—suck the milk from Sethe's breasts. She reports the assault to the ailing Mrs. Garner. The nephews retaliate by beating Sethe with cowhide until her back is split open with wounds. Unknown to Sethe, schoolteacher roasts Sixo alive and hangs Paul A for trying to escape the plantation. Before she leaves Sweet Home, Sethe confronts Paul D, who is shackled in an iron collar for his part in the escape attempt. Sethe then makes her own escape.

Sethe flees through the woods and, with the help of Amy Denver, a runaway white indentured servant, gives birth to her fourth child. Then, with the help of Stamp Paid, a black ferryman, she crosses the Ohio river into freedom.

Safely reunited with her mother-in-law, Baby Suggs, and her babies in Cincinnati, Sethe enjoys 28 days of contentment. Then one day as Stamp Paid replenishes the woodpile and Baby Suggs and Sethe work in the yard, schoolteacher, the sheriff, a slave catcher, and one of schoolteacher's nephews arrive to recapture Sethe and her children. To spare her children a return to bondage, Sethe slices the throat of the eldest girl, tries to kill her two boys, and threatens to dash out the brains of her infant daughter, Denver. The sheriff takes Sethe and Denver to jail, and Sethe is condemned to hang. She leaves her cell long enough to attend her daughter's funeral. Three months later, pressure from the Quaker abolitionist Edward Bodwin and the Colored Ladies of Delaware, Ohio produces Sethe's freedom. She barters sex for a gravestone inscribed "Beloved" to mark her daughter's burial site. Immediately, Beloved's ghost makes itself known in Baby Suggs's house at 124 Bluestone Road.

Sethe is granted a release from her death sentence, but after leaving jail she finds the black community closed to her. With the aid of Mr. Bodwin, she locates work and manages to build a stable, though solitary, life. Her mother-in-law withdraws completely from the community and dies several years later. Shortly after Baby Suggs's death, Sethe's sons leave home, unnerved by the presence of Beloved's ghost. Left with only Denver, Sethe lives in uneasy solitude.

Years later, after escaping a cruel Georgia prison and wandering North, Paul D arrives in Cincinnati and reunites with Sethe. He immediately banishes the disruptive ghost from the house. The two former slaves attempt to form a family, although Denver is uncomfortable with Paul D's presence. Sethe and Paul D's relationship is interrupted by the appearance of a mysterious young woman who calls herself Beloved, the same name that is on the headstone of Sethe's murdered daughter.

Beloved quickly becomes a dominant force in Sethe's house. She drives Paul D out of Sethe's bed and seduces him. She becomes the sole focus of Sethe's life after Sethe realizes that this young woman is the reincarnation of her dead child. Drawing Sethe into an unhealthy, obsessive relationship, Beloved grows stronger while Sethe's body and mind weaken. Sethe quits her job and withdraws completely into the house. With the aid of Denver and some female neighbors, Sethe escapes Beloved's control through a violent scene in which she mistakes Bodwin for a slave catcher and tries to stab him with an ice pick. Beloved vanishes, and Paul D returns, helping Sethe rediscover the value of life and her own self-worth.

List of Characters

Sethe   A former slave whose love for her children and hatred of slavery causes her to commit an unthinkable act in order to keep her children free from a life of bondage.

Beloved   Sethe's third child and oldest daughter who was killed at the age of two. Her restless spirit haunts the family first as a ghost and then as a flesh-and-blood woman.

Denver   Sethe's fourth and youngest child. Traumatized as a young girl by what she discovers about her mother, she grows up lonely and isolated, focusing her love and devotion on Beloved's spirit.

Paul D Garner   A former slave from Sweet Home who survived the horrors of slavery and has evolved into a resourceful, contemplative man. He challenges Sethe to try to make a future with him.

Halle Suggs   Sethe's husband and the youngest of Baby Suggs's eight children. For years, Halle hires himself out to buy his mother's freedom. Although he plans to escape to freedom, the escape plot is discovered and halted by the Sweet Home overseer (schoolteacher). Halle is never heard from again.

Baby Suggs (Jenny Whitlow)   Sethe's mother-in-law. Baby becomes a preacher after Halle buys her freedom, and she provides a stabilizing force for Sethe and Denver.

Buglar and Howard   Sethe and Halle's sons who are frightened by their mother and by Beloved's ghost. They leave home shortly after Baby Suggs's death and never return.

Stamp Paid (Joshua)   The former slave who ferries Sethe and Denver across the Ohio River to freedom and later rescues Denver from being killed.

Vashti   Stamp Paid's wife who, while a slave, was forced to become her master's mistress.

Amy Denver   A young white girl and indentured slave who cares for Sethe when Sethe runs from Sweet Home. She helps deliver Sethe's fourth child, and Sethe names the baby Denver in her honor.

Mr. Garner   The owner of Sweet Home who treats his slaves humanely.

Mrs. Lillian Garner   Mr. Garner's wife who treats both Baby Suggs and Sethe kindly and gives Sethe a pair of crystal earrings as a wedding gift. After Mr. Garner dies, she becomes ill and turns Sweet Home over to her cruel brother-in-law, the schoolteacher.

schoolteacher   The widower of Mr. Garner's sister who takes control of Sweet Home after Mr. Garner's death. He is fascinated with studying the characteristics and behaviors of the Sweet Home slaves, viewing them as animals that can earn him profit.

Sixo   A Sweet Home slave who maintains a relationship with the Thirty-Mile Woman. He is burned alive when captured trying to escape the plantation.

The Thirty-Mile Woman (Patsy)   Sixo's lover who joins the group running from Sweet Home and escapes capture when the others are caught.

Paul A Garner   A Sweet Home slave who is close to Halle and Paul D and plots with them to escape.

Ma'am   Sethe's unnamed mother who was taken from Africa. The hard labor she is subjected to prevents her from spending time with Sethe, and she is killed when Sethe is just a girl.

Nan   The one-armed plantation wet-nurse who crossed the ocean in the same ship that carried Sethe's mother. Nan is a sort of surrogate mother to Sethe, breastfeeding her after the "whitebabies" are fed.

Paul F Garner   One of Sweet Home's three Pauls who is sold to an unspecified owner shortly after Mr. Garner's death so Mrs. Garner has money to run the plantation.

Whitlow   Baby Suggs's former owner in Carolina who named her Jenny Whitlow on the bill of sale.

Hi Man   The black convict in the Georgia prison with Paul D who signals that other inmates can rise from their kneeling position, shuffle off on their common chain, and begin the day's work.

Mr. and Mrs. Buddy   Amy Denver's master and mistress. Mr. Buddy, as vicious as a slave overseer, is said to "whip you for looking at him straight."

Ella   One of Baby Suggs's neighbors in Cincinnati who escorts Sethe and Denver from the riverbank to Baby Suggs's house when they first arrive. Years later, she organizes the local women to exorcise Beloved from the house.

Janey Wagon   A house servant in the Bodwin home.

Lady Jones   A woman of mixed heritage and neighbor of Baby Suggs who offers lessons to the neighborhood children. She later helps Denver climb out of poverty.

Reverend Pike   A minister of the Church of the Redeemer.

Sawyer   A Cincinnati restaurant owner who offers work to Sethe.

Edward Bodwin   A generous Quaker supporter of the Underground Railroad who helps Baby Suggs get settled in Cincinnati and later gives Denver a job.

Miss Bodwin   Edwin Bodwin's unmarried sister who also supports abolition.

Nelson Lord   Denver's schoolmate who ends Denver's education by asking her about Sethe's past.

A Brief Chronology of the Events in *Beloved*

Because Toni Morrison structures her narrative in circular form, events are revealed through the chance offerings of various speakers, usually long after the fact and out of time order. The following retelling of the plot restructures the events in approximate chronology, including certain historical events that support the plot.

1795   Baby Suggs, a slave, is born.

1803   Ohio becomes a state.

1805   Edward Bodwin is born.

1808   The Bodwin family moves from Bluestone Road to Court Street.

1818   Tyree and John, Baby Suggs's sons, run away.

1835   Sethe is born to "Ma'am" in either Carolina or Louisiana. Halle is born. Paul D arrives at Sweet Home.

1838   The Garners learn of the Bodwins' kindness toward ex-slaves. Garner purchases Baby Suggs and Halle.

1848   Sethe arrives at Sweet Home in Pulaski County, Kentucky to replace Baby Suggs, whose freedom Halle has purchased with voluntary weekend work.

1849   Mrs. Garner agrees to Halle's marriage to Sethe. Sethe secretly sews a "bedding dress" from pillow cases, a dresser scarf, and mosquito netting.

        Saturday: Halle consummates his marriage to Sethe in the cornfield.

        Sunday: Mrs. Garner presents Sethe with crystal earrings as a wedding gift.

1850   Baby Suggs finds out that Halle's new wife is about to give birth to their first child, Howard.

        September 18: Congress passes a compromise bill containing a Fugitive Slave Law, intended to appease both slave and free states.

1851   Buglar, Sethe's second son, is born.

        A 20-year period of northern migration for runaway and newly emancipated blacks begins.

        After Mr. Garner's death, Mrs. Garner sells Paul F. (From the proceeds of the sale, she lives two years before summoning schoolteacher and his boys to help her run Sweet Home.)

1854   Beloved, Halle and Sethe's third child and first daughter, is born in November.

1855   Baby Suggs intuitively selects 1855 as the year that Halle died. The Society of Friends is at the height of its abolitionist drive. The Sweet Home slaves unsuccessfully try to escape. Sethe is assaulted by the schoolteacher's nephews before she finally escapes slavery.

Monday: Sethe fears that Halle is dead. Amy helps deliver Denver in a lean-to near the Ohio River. Stamp Paid ferries the pair to a hut. Ella leads them to 124 Bluestone Road, where Baby Suggs tends Sethe's mutilated body.

Four weeks later: Stamp Paid delivers two buckets of berries to Baby Suggs, who expands the gift into a feast for 90 people.

The next day: Sethe kills her oldest daughter and tries to kill her other children when the schoolteacher and his nephews arrive to take her and the children back to Sweet Home. Sethe and Denver are taken to jail.

1856   Paul D is locked onto a chain for 83 days in a prison camp in Albert, Georgia.

1857   *January:* Mudslides force the Albert, Georgia convicts to flee to a Cherokee camp.

February: Paul D starts to migrate north.

July: Paul D arrives in Delaware and moves in with a "weaver lady."

1858   With help from Mr. Bodwin, Sethe gets a job in the kitchen of Sawyer's restaurant.

1860   *January:* Paul D takes a job with the Northpoint Bank and Railroad Company and departs Delaware.

1862   Denver attends Lady Jones's school.

1863   Nelson Lord ends Denver's school days by questioning her about Sethe's jail term.

1864   Denver hears the crawling ghost on the stairs.

Christmas: Miss Bodwin buys cologne for Sethe and Denver, a shawl for Baby Suggs, and oranges for the boys.

1865   Buglar and Howard leave home. Baby Suggs dies before the surrender at Appomattox Courthouse, which occurs April 9. Denver misses her grandmother and urges Sethe to move away from Bluestone Road.

1866   Paul D finds work in Trenton, New Jersey.

1869   Paul D watches five women and fourteen little girls arrive in Rochester and search out a "preacher on DeVore Street."

1873   *Monday in August:* Paul D comes to 124 Bluestone Road in Cincinnati.

         Thursday at 11:00 a.m.: Paul D escorts Denver and Sethe to the carnival beside the lumberyard.

         Thursday afternoon, late: Beloved appears in the flesh, sitting on a stump outside Sethe's house. Sethe loses bladder control.

         Monday: As Denver hovers, Beloved awakens in the keeping room.

         Thursday: Beloved notices the orange patches on the quilt.

         Four weeks after Beloved's arrival: Beloved asks about Sethe's mother and about Sethe's "diamond earrings."

         Five weeks after Beloved's arrival: Paul D presses Beloved for personal information. He reveals to Sethe that Halle observed the schoolteacher's nephews maul and molest her before her escape from Sweet Home.

         By fall: Paul D moves out of Sethe's bed.

         In winter: Beloved seduces Paul D.

         Three weeks later: Paul D feels guilty about his infidelity. He meets Sethe at Sawyer's restaurant intending to confess, but instead he asks her to bear his child.

1874   Stamp Paid reads a newspaper clipping to Paul D that tells the story of Beloved's murder. Paul D confronts Sethe about her deed and then leaves 124 Bluestone Rd. For six consecutive days, Stamp Paid approaches Sethe's door, each time leaving without knocking.

1875   *January:* Denver, Beloved, and Sethe play and enjoy each other's company on the frozen creek.

         March: Sethe discovers the scar on Beloved's neck, which was created when Sethe killed her. By the end of the month, Sethe spends her life savings on fancy food and clothes in an attempt to appease Beloved.

         April: Denver asks Lady Jones for work. Lady Jones gives her food.

A Friday in summer: Thirty women approach 124 Blue-stone Road as Edwin Bodwin comes to fetch Denver to go to work. Thinking Bodwin intends to take her children, Sethe tries to stab him with an ice pick. Ella stops her, and Denver wrestles her to the ground. A very pregnant Beloved vanishes from the porch.

In the days or weeks that follow Beloved's disappearance: Sethe takes to her bed. Paul D returns and helps her learn to live again.

Character Map

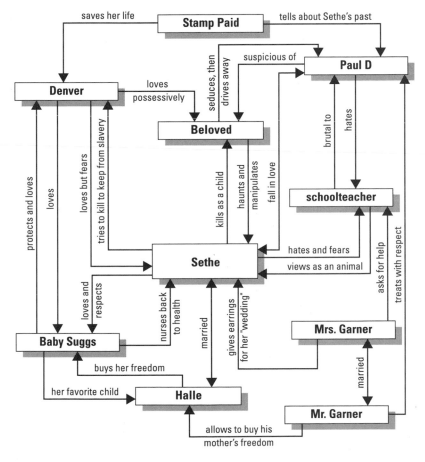

CRITICAL COMMENTARIES

Epigraph. 23

Chapter 1. 24

Chapter 2. 28

Chapter 3. 30

Chapter 4. 33

Chapter 5. 35

Chapter 6. 37

Chapter 7. 39

Chapter 8. 42

Chapter 9. 45

Chapter 10. 48

Chapter 11. 51

Chapter 12. 53

Chapters 13 and 14 56

Chapter 15. 59

Chapter 16. 61

Chapters 17 and 18 63

Chapter 19. 66

Chapters 20 and 21 71

Chapters 22 and 23 73

Chapter 24. 75

Chapter 25. 78

Chapter 26 80

Chapter 27. 85

Chapter 28. 87

Epigraph

In Romans 9, Paul, the spokesperson for Jesus to the developing churches around the Mediterranean shores, writes a stream of letters to remind evolving Christians that they receive God's love through grace. Although they are a rebellious, unruly people, God bestows glory on them out of love for people who are not truly "beloved." Morrison's *epigraph,* or introductory citation, is a fitting opening for a novel about grace, love, and forgiveness. The epigraph sets the tone for the opening chapter, in which a willful ghost destroys the peace of Sethe's home—a home that is free of slavery but still laden with servitude's emotional freight. Paul's words, wrathful and forbidding in certain respects, also contain a promise: "For he will finish the work, and cut it short in righteousness: because a short work will the Lord make upon the earth." In layman's language, either shape up or ship out, because God is coming back for the true believers, gathering them up, and taking them to heaven with speed and finality.

Part One
Chapter 1

Summary

In 1873, Sethe, a former slave, resides with Denver, her reclusive 18-year-old daughter, in a haunted two-story house at 124 Bluestone Road outside of Cincinnati, Ohio. The house once sheltered a close family, including Grandma Baby Suggs; Sethe's two sons, Buglar and Howard; and her infant daughter, Beloved. All are gone now except Sethe and Denver.

Almost nine years after Baby Suggs's death, Sethe and Denver's isolation is ruptured by the unforeseen arrival of Paul D, a survivor of Sweet Home, the Kentucky slave farm where Sethe, her husband Halle, and their children were also enslaved. In conversation, Sethe and Paul D reveal memories of their former lives of subjugation. Owned for years by the benign Garners, a childless couple, the slaves eventually fell under the cruel tyranny of an unnamed schoolteacher, who destroyed the farm's harmony and forced the slaves to desperate measures of rebellion and flight.

Sethe divulges to Paul D the catastrophic events that caused her to run away from Sweet Home. Pregnant with her fourth child and fearing for her family's future under the schoolteacher's reign, Sethe surrendered her sons and daughter to a woman in a wagon, waiting in the corn. Before she could escape herself, however, two white boys—the schoolteacher's nephews—sucked out her breast milk and lashed her with rawhide whips. Although she was in terrible pain from the whipping, Sethe ran away from Sweet Home that night. A white girl found Sethe, tended to her injuries, and helped her give birth to her second daughter.

Sethe reveals that later, her oldest girl died from having her throat cut. Paul D, empathetic because of his own experience with slavery, massages the thick scars on Sethe's back as his other hand strokes her breast. The ghost of Sethe's dead daughter, which haunts her house, reacts angrily to Sethe and Paul D's closeness and causes the whole house to shake. Paul D authoritatively banishes the ghost and takes Sethe to bed. Denver, meanwhile, sits on the porch, missing the ghost's presence and resenting Paul D's intrusion into her and her mother's lives. She miserably appeases her loneliness and apprehension with bread and jelly.

Commentary

Veiled in what Anne Tyler calls the "gauzy mists of magic," *Beloved* opens with the house number 124, a repeated mantra that suggests many numerological possibilities. On one symbolic level, the numbers 1 + 2 + 4 add up to 7, the number of letters on Beloved's headstone. In Christian lore, the number 7 represents charity, grace, and the Holy Spirit, as well as completion and perfection. As we will see later in the novel, Beloved's death signified the end of all of these elements in both Sethe's life and the life of her family. When Beloved died, the family lost the charity of the townspeople, the grace of a happy life together, and Baby Suggs's connection to the Holy Spirit. The family became incomplete and imperfect. The number 124 emphasizes this incompleteness when examined sequentially. The number 3 is missing from the sequence, just as Sethe's third child is missing from the family. A more complicated arithmetic equation denotes Sethe's arrival at Sweet Home and her selection of Halle as her husband, an act that leads to four children, doubling of one into two and two into four.

Chapter 1 introduces a number of *motifs* (repeating ideas or images) that support Morrison's themes. In addition to numbers, the most significant motifs that reappear in later chapters are these:

■ Bestiality, or having animal-like characteristics. This motif is demonstrated by references to the "baby's venom" and Sethe being down "on all fours." References that appear later in the novel include Sethe calling her unborn child a "little antelope" and Garner's slaves copulating with calves.

■ Colors, particularly the "gray and white house on Bluestone Road" and the white stairs that lead to the bedrooms on the second floor.

■ Plants, especially the clinging chamomile sap that Sethe hurries to rinse from her legs, the cherry gum and oak bark used for making ink, and the sycamore trees that become gallows for hanging slaves. The poignant touch of the chokeberry tree on Sethe's back compels the reader to empathize with her suffocating misery.

■ Breastfeeding, a central issue, which provides Sethe's infant with food and the ravaging white boys a source of mammary rape.

■ The heart, a welcoming, nurturing image implied by the "pool of red and undulating light" that invites Paul D to settle into Sethe's house. Red becomes Beloved's signature and is the hue that Baby Suggs avoided late in life when she focused only on colors.

■ Iron, a dual symbol that describes Sethe's eyes and backbone and also represents Paul D's bondage in two torture devices, one bridling his tongue and another collaring him with outstretched tines (prongs) so that he couldn't lie down or lean back in comfort.

■ Superstition, indicated by Paul D's awareness of the ghost baby and his reference to the "headless bride," as well as Denver's memories of her brothers telling her "die-witch! stories."

■ Female genitalia, briefly implied by women "way past the Change of Life" (menopause).

■ Resurrection, the hopeful image implicit in the "dawn-colored stone studded with star chips."

Glossary

slop jars indoor containers that take the place of toilets, especially for night use or for people too ill or infirm to walk outside to an outhouse.

Dearly Beloved the traditional opening words for a Protestant wedding or funeral.

chamomile sap juice from any plant of two genera of the composite family, with strong-smelling foliage; esp., a plant whose dried, daisylike flower heads are used as a medicine and in making tea.

hazelnut stranger a visitor with reddish-brown skin.

pouch of tobacco ... smoking paper the materials needed for hand-rolling cigarettes.

chokecherry a North American wild cherry tree yielding an astringent fruit.

Sethe took a little spit from the tip of her tongue . . . lightly she touched the stove   a method of testing temperature in a wood-stove. A skillful cook can detect by the sizzle of saliva when a stove is hot enough for baking.

I had milk   an unusual occurrence that Sethe is both pregnant and lactating, since breastfeeding suppresses ovulation. Also, the likelihood that a woman can endure extreme trauma and still produce milk for two children is a rare example of determination winning out over cruel circumstances.

pass her air   to burp.

wire from the top of the jar and then the lid   a forerunner of the metal-lidded canning jar. The container was sealed when the wire bail was pulled into place at the top of the glass lid.

cloth . . . cake of wax   a method of sealing jelly to prevent mold and keep out insects.

die witch! stories   scary tales that Denver's brothers told her, suggesting their fear of Sethe, who had tried to execute them.

keeping room   a colonial term for parlor or sitting room.

Part One
Chapter 2

Summary

The brief and unsatisfying sexual encounter between Paul D and Sethe reminds them both of slavery. He recalls his slave-brother, Sixo, who walked 34 miles to and from meetings with his lover, Patsy; Sethe recalls kitchen work for Mrs. Garner, who helped her with the tedious chores of bristle-sorting and ink-making. Aged 13 when she arrived at Sweet Home, Sethe took a year to select a husband from among the five male slaves. Halle, the gentlest man, revealed his qualities through devotion to Baby Suggs, his crippled mother, whom he worked to emancipate. Sethe naively requested a marriage service to honor her union with Halle. Mrs. Garner laughed a little at the suggestion of slaves needing the same type of marital conventions as whites. Nonetheless, Sethe, dressed in a make-do wedding frock, enjoyed her brief honeymoon in Mr. Garner's cornfield. The other Sweet Home slaves celebrated Sethe and Halle's honeymoon evening with a feast of new corn.

Commentary

From the start of Sethe's relationship with Paul D, she recognizes the difference between their passion and the brother-sister love that she and Halle shared. While Sethe and Paul D begin their relationship within a reality haunted by the pain of the past, Sethe and Halle's relationship blossomed in the pastoral setting of Sweet Home, surrounded by the mythic trappings of Eden, a tree-lined haven where the indigo-black Sixo walked naked and danced at night in the emancipating groves. Whereas Sethe and Paul D make love openly in the middle of the day, Sethe and Halle, who rose early and went to bed late, had limited time for love on weekdays and looked forward to the luxury of gazing at each other on Sundays, their day of blessing and communion.

Literary Device

Replete with physical, visual, oral, and auditory impressions, the extended metaphor of the cornfield blends two motifs—plants and female genitalia. The clinical revelation of Sethe's clitoris ("parting the hair to get to the tip, the edge of his fingernail just under, so as not to grace a single kernel") and the glans of Halle's penis ("pulling down of the tight sheath") gives way to gentle, virginal images of the "ear [yielding] up to him its shy rows, exposed at last." Morrison, entranced with the image, repeats "How loose the silk," suggesting the girlish sweetness of Sethe, whose pubic hair is still "fine and loose and free." Their union is favorable to the lovers, because its "simple joy" meets their anticipations.

Glossary

pitched ceiling   an angled ceiling with windows opening on the sky.

indigo   a deep violet blue.

salsify   a purple-flowered plant of the composite family, with long, white, edible, fleshy roots having an oysterlike flavor.

butter wouldn't come   the cream failed to clot into butter.

brine in the barrel   a primitive method of preserving fish, meat, and vegetables. The salt draws out the natural juices and replaces them with brine, or water full of salt, which impedes spoilage.

myrtle   a plant with evergreen leaves, white or pinkish flowers, and dark, fragrant berries.

bristle   any short, stiff, prickly hair of an animal or plant.

mint sprig   a piece of an aromatic plant whose leaves are used for flavoring and in medicine; a natural breath freshener.

Brother   a favorite tree at Sweet Home.

Part One

Chapter 3

Summary

A solitary child-woman, Denver takes refuge in a circle of boxwood shrubs and inhales the fragrance of cologne. Her memories return to an earlier time when she saw Sethe kneeling in prayer beside a white dress with "its sleeve around her mother's waist." Denver savors the story of her birth and Sethe's dim memories of her own mother, known only as Ma'am. Denver's thoughts blend with Sethe's voice retelling the episode in which Sethe prepared to die but was saved by Amy Denver, a threadbare white servant girl fleeing toward Boston from the cruelties of Mr. Buddy. Amy's plucky encouragement and application of first aid relieved Sethe's swollen feet and helped her crawl to safety, far from schoolteacher's reach.

Chiming in is a third voice, Paul D. Paul D is singing prison songs and thinking over his journey from Sweet Home to Alfred, Georgia and on to Delaware. Hinting that he may settle in Cincinnati, Paul D asks Sethe about job opportunities and questions whether Denver will mind his presence. Sethe, who believes that Denver is a charmed child, begins telling Paul D how schoolteacher tracked her family down in Cincinnati. She indicates that she spent time in jail after schoolteacher's visit and that Denver remained safely with her when she was imprisoned.

Commentary

Literary Device

Morrison's use of a complex circular narrative technique squeezes out bits of information from various viewpoints, none of which supplies the whole picture. The bits of information, which form the outline of a *gestalt,* or pattern, create enough clarity to elicit suspense in the reader, who must remain in tune as Sethe holds back crucial information and Denver continues to anticipate some undefined connection with the past. Sethe makes plain to Paul D that Denver is the center of her life and the sole concern of her daily existence. Her brief comment that the jail rats "bit everything in there but her" delineates the extent of Sethe's protection. Sketchy details, deliberately chosen for maximum concealment, obscure the story between the arrival of slave catchers at 124 Bluestone Road and Sethe's incarceration in a cell. Meanwhile, the charmed protection that Sethe describes Denver as having seems symbolically represented in the ring of boxwood bushes that Denver enters to escape from loneliness. Denver's green retreat, another Edenic symbol, suggests a religious treatment of the spot where her grandmother once preached.

The description of Denver being born in a vaginal-shaped canoe adds to the motif of genital images. Imagining herself delivered on the river that divides slavery and freedom pleases the girl because the event epitomizes Sethe's devotion to motherhood.

Character Insight

The burden of painful memories for both Sethe and Paul D produces typically female and male responses. Sethe, like the house, covers herself in a breastplate of silence as a means of shielding Denver from earlier horrors. Paul D, the intruding male figure in a female-dominated environment, sings away his troubles with restless, urgent, masculine verses recalling hunger, labor, weariness, and a controlled impulse to avenge himself on the overseer. Realizing that his macho lyrics are out of place, Paul D turns his pent-up energies to the repair of the broken window and table leg. His supportive presence results in a tenuous harmony within the household as he ponders settling into a steady job and family life.

Glossary

wild veronica   any of a genus of plants of the figwort family, with white or bluish flower spikes.

cold house   a springhouse or storage shed for dairy items, meats, and other items which would spoil in a hot kitchen.

privy   a toilet; esp., an outhouse.

watery field   terrain flooded for the cultivation of rice.

bloody side of the Ohio River   Kentucky. The Ohio River separated Kentucky, a slave state, and Ohio, a free state.

huckleberries   the fruit of any of a genus of plants of the heath family, having dark-blue berries with ten large seeds.

carmine   red or purplish-red; crimson.

foal to give birth to (a foal). By comparing Sethe's condition to that of a pregnant mare, Amy reveals white prejudice about blacks, whom owners treated like brood animals so that their offspring, like foals or piglets or calves, could be reared for labor or for market.

lisle a fabric, or stockings, gloves, etc., knit or woven of lisle, a fine, hard, extra-strong cotton thread.

molly apple the wild fruit of a perennial woodland plant of the barberry family, with shield-shaped leaves and a single, large, white, cuplike flower.

glazing the work of a glazier in fitting windows, etc. with glass.

Part One
Chapter 4

Summary

After three days, Denver demands to know whether Paul D intends to stay. Sethe insists that Paul D remain and scolds Denver for discourtesy, even though the girl is old enough to be considered an adult. To ease the tension, Paul D invites Sethe and Denver to go to a carnival, saying "Thursday, tomorrow, is for coloreds . . . ." The next morning, the threesome, among Cincinnati's 400 blacks, walk toward the lumberyard and take in the sights, including clowns and freaks.

Commentary

Morrison uses this small chapter to develop both plot and mood. Paul D, who has no understanding of Sethe's sufferings during their 18 years apart or her intense relationship with her one remaining child, probes for the unspoken admission of her affection for him. At the same time, he knows enough of the post-slavery era to realize that it's dangerous for a "used-to-be-slave woman to love anything that much." Innocent of the hurt that Sethe conceals, he manfully promises to "catch you 'fore you fall."

During the morning's entertainment at the carnival ("Pickaninnies free!"), Paul D redeems himself with both women by spending his last two dollars on treats while they watch the Snake Charmer, an Arabian Nights dancer, the Fat Lady, and other sights. Their shadows appear to link hands as they walk, which Sethe takes as a positive omen. However, the overall atmosphere of the morning's jaunt is tainted by images of danger, juncture, violence, savagery, and dismemberment, as the carnival entertainers are "eating glass, swallowing fire, spitting ribbons, twisted into knots, forming pyramids, playing with snakes and beating each other up." The carnival, an embodiment of illusion, serves as entertainment. However, the images in this chapter foreshadow the time when Sethe must reveal to Denver and Paul D the vile memories that refuse to exonerate her. Like the snake of Eden, something evil coils in wait.

Glossary

croaker sack   a burlap bag.

walking man   an unsettled man, not the marrying kind.

pickaninnies   black children. The term, derived from Spanish or Portuguese, evolved into a racial slur meant to denigrate or dehumanize.

horehound   candy made with horehound juice, a bitter juice extracted from a horehound herb's leaves, stem, or flowers.

Part One
Chapter 5

Summary

As Paul D, Sethe, and Denver return from the carnival late Thursday afternoon, they encounter a lone young woman, wet and wheezing, who has walked up from the stream and is napping on the stump outside the house. To Paul's questions, the girl gives hazy responses, introducing herself as Beloved and denying that she has a last name. Concerned for her tenuous state of health, Sethe and Paul D take her in; Denver quivers with anticipation. The girl sleeps for four days in Baby Suggs's former room. Paul D fears that Beloved may suffer from cholera. Denver takes care of her, hiding Beloved's urine-soaked sheets and lying about the fact that Beloved appears weak on her feet even though she is able to lift a rocking chair with one hand.

Commentary

Literary Device

Morrison liberally salts this chapter with details that indicate that the visitor is the embodiment of Sethe's daughter Beloved, who would be about 20 years old if she had lived. Tendrils of superstition cling to the scene, such as the following:

- Beloved emerges from the water, like a child born from a watery sac.

- Her wobbly head is reminiscent of a newborn unable to support the weight of its oversized cranium. In this book, it is also emblematic of a head partially severed from the neck.

- Beloved's unlined hands and baby-soft complexion are as fragile as the skin of an infant.

- Her extreme thirst suggests a baby eager to nurse.

- The disappearance of the dog, Here Boy, is a gothic touch springing from traditions that claim animals can sense the presence of evil.

■ Sethe's loss of bladder control is an image of the emptying of the chorion and amnion preceding birth.

It seems strange that Sethe, who often thinks about her dead daughter and has lived with her daughter's ghost for years, fails to connect the girl's name with her own Beloved. However, perhaps the idea that her daughter might return to her as something other than a spirit is something that Sethe cannot conceive. When Denver displays uncharacteristic devotion toward Beloved, Sethe assumes that Denver's compassion arises from a need for female companionship near her own age. Denver, perceiving that Beloved is the "something" that she has been waiting for, demonstrates her understanding of who Beloved is by announcing that Here Boy is not going to return.

The events in this chapter establish the foundation for the four-way emotional conflict that will arise as the novel continues. These events will ultimately lead to Denver's emancipation from an overprotective mother and Sethe's confrontation with her secret past. Meanwhile, cautiously silent Paul D will navigate the troubled waters between mother and daughters and realize that the expansion of a triad (Sethe, Denver, and Paul D) into a foursome (Sethe, Beloved, Denver, and Paul D) greatly weakens his position as the evolving male head of the household.

Glossary

looking for something to beat a life of tobacco and sorghum Paul D assumes that the stranger is a farm girl, fleeing the labor-intensive chores associated with the production of tobacco and molasses.

talking sheets members of the Ku Klux Klan, who hide their identity beneath white sheets.

croup a condition resulting from any obstruction of the larynx, esp. an inflammation of the respiratory passages, with labored breathing, hoarse coughing, and laryngeal spasm.

He won't be back Here Boy leaves because dogs are believed to sense the presence of a ghost.

Part One
Chapter 6

Summary

In the fourth week of her residency at 124 Bluestone Road, Beloved clings to Sethe, following her about the kitchen and awaiting her return from work at the restaurant. Like a hungry child, Beloved clamors for Sethe's stories, questioning her about her "diamonds," the crystal earrings that Mrs. Garner gave Sethe as a wedding gift to mark the union that had no proper ceremony or celebration. Sethe describes how she pilfered fabrics to fashion a wedding dress, which she topped off with a wool shawl that "kept [her] from looking like a haint peddling." Following the Saturday honeymoon in the cornfield, Mrs. Garner gave Sethe the earrings and wished the couple happiness.

More questions about Sethe's mother elicit meager facts—that she worked in indigo fields from dawn to nightfall and then slept through Sundays. The demands of her toil gave her only a few weeks in which to bond with her infant daughter, who was then passed on to a wet-nurse so that Ma'am could return to the fields. Once, Ma'am carried Sethe behind the smokehouse and lifted her breast to reveal a circle and cross burned into her flesh so that the child could always identify her mother. After her mother was hanged, Sethe examined her corpse but was unable to locate the symbols on the decaying flesh.

Retelling the vile stories forces Sethe to abandon narrative and move into action. Lifting damp sheets, she begins folding them as she tries to answer Beloved's insistent queries about Ma'am. Sethe can recall only that many slaves were killed along with her mother, and that Nan, a one-armed black governess, took over the role of parent and taught Sethe her mother's native dialect. Pained by the sorrowful "rememory," Sethe longs for the comfort of her mother-in-law, Baby Suggs. To Denver's relief, Sethe shifts her attention from the tense conversation to the imminent arrival of Paul D.

Commentary

Character Insight

The relationship between Sethe and Beloved, which will later turn sadomasochistic, begins innocently with storytelling, the oral tradition that forms the core of black history and black literature. Violating her unspoken pact with Baby Suggs to leave memories of slave days out of conversation, Sethe "[gives] short replies or rambling incomplete reveries" in response to Beloved's many questions. Her memories cause her pain in exchange for Beloved's pleasure. Like the pull of an infant mouth on a mother's tender breast, Beloved's intense delight in Sethe's past seems to nourish an inner need to know more about the crystal earrings and about Ma'am, Beloved's unnamed grandmother.

Literary Device

Offsetting the hurt of child to mother is Sethe's massaging of Denver's wet hair with a towel. A motif introduced by Paul D's reverent touching of Sethe's scarred back in the first chapter and by Amy's attentions to her swollen feet when she first escaped from Sweet Home, the concept of a healing touch evolves in later chapters into a powerful message. The characters, who are incapable of obliterating the hurtful memories of enslavement, minister to each other in imperfect human fashion, applying fingers and hands as a kind of tangible blessing, flesh to flesh. Together with the repeated image of breastfeeding, Morrison frequently delineates methods by which one human being comforts another.

Glossary

familiar   in folklore, an evil spirit constantly attending someone and typically viewed as dwelling within an animal; also, the animal within which such a spirit dwells.

fast bread   bread made from batter rather than yeast dough, which must rise before it can be baked.

half peck   a unit of dry measure equal to an eighth of a bushel, or four quarts.

the bit   the part of a bridle that goes into a horse's mouth, used to control the horse; in this context, it is used by plantation overseers to bridle a slave's tongue.

night bucket   the slop jar or portable night toilet.

press   an upright closet in which clothes or other articles are kept.

haint   a dialect pronunciation of "haunt;" a ghost.

in line   the positioning of slave teams to work the indigo fields.

Part One
Chapter 7

Summary

At the end of five weeks, Beloved, who is hesitant to reveal personal information, gives a clue to her past—the fact that she "was at the bridge." Sethe halts Paul D's intrusive grilling about how Beloved could have walked a long way without soiling her new shoes. Beloved bursts out in baby talk: "I take the shoes! I take the dress! The shoe strings don't fix!" Denver, recognizing that Beloved has never learned to tie a bow, promises to teach her.

Paul D, uneasy about the glow that illuminates Beloved, concludes that there is some significance to the girl's arrival on the very day that Sethe and he had "patched up their quarrel, gone out in public and had a right good time—like a family." Just as he determines to investigate Beloved, she chokes on a raisin and then says she wants to go to sleep. Delighted to have an intimate companion, Denver escorts her to the upstairs bedroom.

Sethe and Paul D, left to themselves, discuss his vexation with Beloved. Paul D boasts that he "never mistreated a woman." Sethe indicates that Halle mistreated her by leaving his children. Paul D shocks Sethe by revealing that on the night the schoolteacher's nephews assaulted her and stole her breast milk, Halle was hidden in the barn loft and saw the attack take place. Traumatized by his wife's suffering, Halle lost his mind, and the last time Paul D saw him, he was sitting mutely with butter smeared all over his face. Paul D could not cry out at the horror of this image because his own mouth was stifled by an iron bit as he waited for transportation to a labor camp in Alfred, Georgia.

Sethe, her image of the loving Halle shattered by this revelation, boils over with rage at the menacing "boys with mossy teeth," schoolteacher taking notes during the assault, and Halle watching from the loft but taking no action to defend her. She calms herself by examining Paul D's face, which is somehow free of the wildness that afflicts most men who have suffered the iron bit. Paul D tells Sethe that the worst of his humiliation after being captured by schoolteacher was the glare of Mister, the deformed rooster that he helped hatch from its shell. Sethe, having heard this confession of pain and degradation, massages his knee in sympathy.

Commentary

Literary Device

It is revealed in this chapter that Sethe's house was once a way station. The motif of the way station, a key element in the novel, operates on two levels. As an earthly dwelling for a wandering spirit, Sethe's house serves as Beloved's resting place after she crosses the bridge to return from the afterlife. Historically, the way station was a treasured salvation for ex-slaves who lacked food, clothing, and safe passage among whites. For illiterate blacks who identified themselves by the scraps of names they were presented in slavery, the way station also served as a postal center and message drop. Chance meetings with other wayfarers sometimes reunited them with friends and loved ones. Barring such windfall, the way station provided a warm, dry, and safe rest stop along the wearying road away from slavery.

Character Insight

Paul D, lost in thought, relives his 20 years on the road after leaving Sweet Home, where he encountered "Negroes so stunned, or hungry, or tired or bereft it was a wonder they recalled or said anything." As he and Sethe try to resolve the mystery of Halle's disappearance, Paul D bursts out with a defense of Halle, who epitomizes the emasculated black male, impeded from protecting his family: "A man ain't a goddamn ax. Chopping, hacking busting every goddamn minute of the day. Things get to him. Things he can't chop down because they're inside."

The bestial image of Mister, the regal rooster, smiling from his tub, destroyed Paul D's remaining sense of humanity as he waited to be carted off to prison. He now recognizes the bitter irony of the fact that the bad-tempered rooster was free to be what it was—a rooster—while Paul D was stripped of his human dignity and treated like an animal. He mourns the men of Sweet Home, "one crazy, one sold, one missing, one burnt and me licking iron with my hands crossed behind me." Sethe's maternal response to Paul D is as instinctive as soothing a child. To her, the rubbing and pressing of his anguished limbs brings the satisfaction of bread-making. As Sethe kneads Paul D's bony knee, her mind turns to her restaurant job and the workaday wisdom that there's "nothing better than [kneading bread] to start the day's serious work of beating back the past."

Glossary

way station   a safe house where wandering blacks could inquire about relatives and expect hospitality.

paterollers   patrollers or slave-catchers.

Pulaski County, Kentucky   a county in south central Kentucky.

the dragon   a Klan symbol.

underground agent   the guide who waited in the cornfield to lead slaves to freedom.

clabber   thickly curdled sour milk.

sugar teat   an early kind of pacifier; a small square of cloth filled with a mixture of brown sugar and butter, tied off, and given to babies to suck on.

Part One
Chapter 8

Summary

Enjoying the sisterly companionship of Beloved, Denver sits on the bed and smiles as Beloved dances. Denver questions Beloved's name and her method of escaping the netherworld to see her mother's face once more. Denver begs Beloved not to leave; Beloved retorts that it's Sethe whom she needs—not her sister. Denver tries to soothe Beloved's outburst by retelling the story of how Amy Denver helped Sethe give birth.

Sethe, instinctively wary of telling too much to a white woman who could easily turn in a runaway slave for a reward, had identified herself to Amy as Lu. Unburdened by race prejudice, Amy set about easing Sethe's pain. She hummed as she performed primitive first aid to Sethe's swollen feet and maimed back. She also fashioned slippers from pieces of Sethe's shawl, which she filled with leaves. By noon, Amy and Sethe had reached the Ohio River and located a boat with one oar.

Water seeping into the boat threatened to engulf Sethe in her birthing labor, but she succeeded in delivery on her fourth push. Amy wrapped the infant in her skirt, and the two women waded ashore. At twilight, Amy left, admonishing Sethe to tell the child how "Miss Amy Denver. Of Boston" brought her into the world. Sethe, relaxing into sleep, murmured the name "Denver."

Commentary

Character Insight

Morrison's characterization of Denver reveals a pensiveness, a longing to cancel an old debt. Isolated physically and emotionally by her mother's secrets, she knows only the oral tradition of her birth and other bits of her life story that she has derived over the years. By identifying with Sethe's flight into the woods, Denver is able to feel the dogs following and dread the white men's "mossy teeth" and their guns. Emulating a nursing mother, she thrives on feeding Beloved's curiosity about the past.

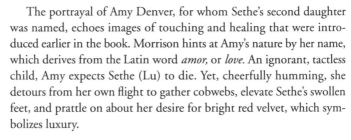

Literary Device

The portrayal of Amy Denver, for whom Sethe's second daughter was named, echoes images of touching and healing that were introduced earlier in the book. Morrison hints at Amy's nature by her name, which derives from the Latin word *amor,* or *love.* An ignorant, tactless child, Amy expects Sethe (Lu) to die. Yet, cheerfully humming, she detours from her own flight to gather cobwebs, elevate Sethe's swollen feet, and prattle on about her desire for bright red velvet, which symbolizes luxury.

Character Insight

The contrast between Amy and Sethe reveals much about the social and economic climate of pre-Civil War America. Amy, who croons three verses of an elegant Renaissance lullaby, may have come from an educated mother. Like Sethe, she cannot identify her father and has endured the whims of a callous master. Unlike Sethe, she fixes her hopes on a future filled with material pleasures. Although Amy, child of an indentured white servant, endured her share of torment from Mr. Buddy, she was spared the black woman's use as a brood animal and knows nothing of the demands of motherhood. Sethe, so far removed from materialism that she fashioned a wedding dress from stolen pillow cases, a scorched scarf, and discolored mosquito netting, sets her hopes on her children, who are her treasures. Whereas Amy has the option to refuse to nurse a child, for Sethe, the act of breast-feeding is the focal point of her drive to stay alive, to deliver the "antelope" kicking her womb, and to cross the river to Cincinnati, where Buglar, Howard, and Beloved await.

As though blessed by "four summer stars," emblematic of her four children, Sethe ignores hunger, pain, and fear in her rush to get milk to her baby. An equivalent number of contractions bring Denver safely to life before the foundering boat almost submerges both mother and child.

Literary Device

In benediction, Morrison blesses Sethe's "charmed" daughter (Denver) with a sprinkling of bluefern spores, the "seeds in which the whole generation sleeps confident of a future." This blessing uses the *pathetic fallacy*—the ascription of human traits or feelings to inanimate nature. It bends nature to the author's purpose, yet, in a leaky boat shaped like a human vulva, it promises no more than momentary safety on the "bloody side of the river."

Glossary

spiderwebs   used as a primitive type of coagulant, or clotting agent.

to let my water   to urinate.

I been bleeding   I have been menstruating.

pike   a highway.

in the brace   in a vise.

to curse His daddy   say "Goddamn."

sunshots   sunlight reflected by water.

Part One
Chapter 9

Summary

The stabilizing influence of Baby Suggs seems far removed from the jarring news of Halle's bizarre splash in the butter churn. No longer anchored by the living presence of her loving mother-in-law, Sethe recalls Baby Suggs's admonition to abandon the past. In the clearing where Baby Suggs once preached, men, women, and children danced, sang, and celebrated the crippled old woman's healing love. Herself defeated by a weak heart, a month after Sethe arrived in Cincinnati, Baby Suggs took to her bed, caressed bright colors, and, blaming "those white things," willed herself to die.

Sethe's mental journey returns her to the Kentucky riverside where Denver was born and where Stamp Paid fed Sethe fried eel and river water from a jar. Because fever gripped her body and dampened the baby, Stamp Paid ordered his nephew to take off his jacket; in it he swaddled the newborn. Stamp Paid then ferried Sethe across the Ohio to an earth-floored shack, marking the sty with a knotted white rag. Responding to the signal, Ella arrived with potatoes, a blanket, cloth, and a pair of men's shoes, which had to be split to accommodate Sethe's swollen feet.

Sethe welcomed the news that her other three children had already arrived at their grandmother's house. Despite Ella's terse advice that she not love anything, Sethe basked in the loving reception she received when she and her newborn arrived at 124 Bluestone Road. She felt true comfort in Baby Suggs's gentle bathing and binding. Baby Suggs stitched a dress for Sethe to wear and, after rescuing Mrs. Garner's crystal earrings from the hem of her old dress, discarded the garments she arrived in. Sethe's older daughter delighted in the jingle of the earrings.

Turning her thoughts to the present, Sethe, accompanied by Denver and Beloved, reaches the clearing and ponders her doubts that Halle will ever return. As she muses about the possibility of life with Paul D, Sethe feels fingers closing around her neck and strangling her. Denver rushes to her aid. When Sethe can breathe again, Beloved massages Sethe's bruised flesh and kisses her. Denver halts the girl's assistance, but not before Sethe momentarily recognizes the touch, which is identical to the touch she once felt from the two-year-old ghost of her daughter. Reflecting further on Paul D's love, Sethe understands Denver's need for a sister.

Sethe plans a tasty dinner for Paul D, who soaks in the tub and gestures to Sethe to join him. Beloved arrives unseen and, filled with jealousy, goes back outside. Denver accuses Beloved of choking Sethe, and Beloved runs to the stream.

Denver thinks about the time she spent when she was seven attending Lady Jones's school, where she made progress in reading and writing until Nelson Lord revealed the reason why neighbors shunned her house: "Didn't your mother get locked away for murder? Wasn't you in there with her when she went?" Two years after Nelson Lord drove her out of school, Denver first heard the sounds of the crawling baby ghost. The spirit's spiteful intrusion unnerved Denver's brothers; to escape the oppressive atmosphere of 124, they left home after Denver's grandmother died.

Back in the present, Denver assesses how she can relieve her agonizing solitude. She turns to her sister, who crouches in the stream and watches two turtles mate.

Commentary

Morrison blends several religious conventions in this chapter. Like Pythia, Apollo's priestess in ancient Delphi, "Baby Suggs, holy" sat in her shrine—the clearing—and, without training, responded intuitively to the spiritual needs of all comers. Her Christ-like message, "Let the children come," emulates Mark 10:14, "Suffer the little children to come unto me." Reaching out to men and women as well, Baby Suggs bid the children to laugh, the men to dance, and the women to cry. The throng, mixing their roles in a symphony of laughter, dance, and sobs, responded to Baby Suggs's "great big heart."

Literary Device

Like the Native American All-Mother or Mediterranean Earth Mother mythic figures who offer blessings and transcend time and place by permeating all cultures, Baby Suggs offers her own version of Christ's beatitudes. After the battering self-denial of slavery, her followers need self-esteem more than theology. Baby Suggs exhorts them to find human comfort—to love their hands and to use them in touching, patting, and stroking others. She names feet, backs, shoulders, arms, liver, and "the prize"—the heart. A foreshadowing of Baby Suggs's heart condition as well as of Sethe's need to rediscover her own self-worth, the scene anticipates the conclusion of the novel in which Sethe, no longer able to lean upon her wise mother-in-law, finds acceptance in Paul D and thus accepts herself.

Sethe's salvation is challenged, however, by a harrowing event that causes the neighboring black community to shun her for 18 years. Coinciding with Baby Suggs's collapse, this event occurs a mere month after Sethe's reunion with her children. The description of the four-week period of peace as "twenty-eight days" reflects another feminine detail, the lunar cycle that governs the menstrual flow.

Glossary

Don't study war no more   a line from "Down By the Riverside." Baby Suggs, an illiterate preacher, took her texts from Negro spirituals.

fixing ceremony   the arrangement of a corpse for burial.

AMEs and Baptists, Holinesses and Sanctifieds   black religious denominations. AMEs refers to the African Methodist Episcopal church, founded in New York City in 1801 by Richard Allen.

buckeyes   the seeds of any of various trees of the horse-chestnut family.

flatbed   a flat-bottomed skiff.

hutch   a hut.

juniper   any of a genus of evergreen shrubs or trees of the cypress family, with needlelike or scalelike foliage, aromatic wood, and berrylike cones that yield an oil used for flavoring gin and formerly in medicine.

rind   a piece of pork skin, traditional southern style seasoning for green beans.

raised bread   yeast bread.

four o'clocks   any of a genus of chiefly American annual or perennial herbs, esp. a garden plant with fragrant yellow, red, or white flowers opening late in the afternoon.

Part One
Chapter 10

Summary

Paul D relives the savage treatment that he endured while shackled to ten other slaves and transported to a brutal prison for the crime of threatening to kill Brandywine, the man who bought him from school-teacher after the attempted escape from Sweet Home. From Kentucky through Virginia and on to Alfred, Georgia, to the underground cell that housed him, Paul D struggled against the despair and dehumanization that accompany forced labor. For example, each morning, the white guards forced the chained row of black men down on their knees, and a few men were chosen to perform oral sex on the guards before beginning the grueling day. Chained in one long line of 46 convicts, Paul D learned the nuances of wordless gestures and expressions and mourned his captivity in song.

Eighty-six days into his sentence, Paul D and the other prisoners, chained together and threatened with suffocation under a mudslide, dived beneath their cells' restraining bars and escaped. The prisoners fled to a Cherokee camp, where Native Americans fed them mush and released them from their leg irons. The scent of their trail was drowned in mud, preventing dogs from tracking them. Secure for the moment, the survivors discussed alternatives. Paul D was the last to make a move. A month after his escape, he headed north and was taken in by a Delaware weaver lady.

Commentary

Morrison, drawing parallels with epic journeys of classical literature, presents a sharp contrast between Paul D's and Sethe's breaks with slavery. Recall that Sethe, her body impelling her toward a nursing baby, moved directly through the forest, crawling to spare her sore, swollen feet, pausing to give birth in a canoe, and ignoring cold, damp, and hunger in her obsessive urge to reunite with Beloved and her boys. Focused solely on her family, Sethe lacked Paul D's drive to put the past behind him, including "Halle, his brothers, Sethe", and the other reminders of Sweet Home.

After his sale to Brandywine and incarceration on a chain gang for attempted murder, Paul D follows the examples of Odysseus, Aeneas, and Jason from Greek mythology by making a meandering tour of escape. The threat of his burial in a mudslide is reminiscent of the forays that Odysseus, Aeneas, and Orpheus made into the underworld. Paul D is rejuvenated by his brief sojourn with Native Americans, who suffered their own share of the white man's hell. Then—like Odysseus's Circe, Jason's Medea, and Aeneas's Dido—an accommodating female weaver took Paul D to bed.

While Sethe enjoyed 28 days of freedom with her family, Paul D, supported by the brotherhood of the pox-ridden Cherokee, had no responsibility, no direction, and no blood ties calling to him. Whereas Sethe was welcomed to freedom by armfuls of babies, kisses, tender strokes on her boys' flesh, and Baby Suggs's healing baths, Paul D had no salve for his lingering psychic pain. The masculine image of the tobacco tin, which he carries in a shirt pocket, becomes the hardened heart that wards off feelings and permanent attachments. Like the box that nearly became his tomb in the convict camp, the tobacco tin entombs his emotions.

Morrison's hasty but touching gesture toward Cherokee sufferings underscores the careful network of details that underlie the story. The history of the Cherokee, replicated throughout white–Indian relations, delineates European greed and racism. The Cherokee, like their black brothers, knew the suffering generated by contact with whites and willingly shared mush, tools, and information about the trail of blossoms that led Paul D to freedom.

Glossary

coffle   a group of animals or slaves fastened together in a line, or driven along together.

taking a bit of foreskin with him to Jesus   biting the guard's penis during fellatio before being shot.

bay or eat my own mess   go mad and howl or eat excrement.

talked through that chain like Sam Morse   communicated through the chain by wordless jerks similar to Morse code.

Georgia took up all of Alabama and Mississippi the taint of slavery made one Deep South state indistinguishable from another.

Alfred possibly Alpharetta, a small Georgia community north of Atlanta.

Sea Islands islands sheltering black communities that cling to African language, customs, and worship.

the river that slid down from the Blue Ridge Mountains the Oconee River.

Oklahoma the destination of 14,000 Cherokee, who in 1838, following the discovery of gold on their lands, were forced to resettle on reservations after a long march named the Trail of Tears. Over 4,000 Cherokee died along the way.

George III King of England during the American Revolution, with whom the Cherokee sided.

published a newspaper Sequoyah's *Cherokee Phoenix,* founded in 1828.

led Oglethorpe through forests native guides helped General James Oglethorpe colonize Georgia in 1733, the same year that he founded Savannah.

helped Andrew Jackson fight Creek the Battle of Horseshoe Bend, March 17, 1814.

King of Spain Charles IV.

been experimented on by Dartmouth refers to the use of blacks and Indians as test animals. These unsuspecting people were infected with syphilis so that health officials could study the progress of the disease.

wrote their language In 1820, Sequoyah invented a phonetic alphabet which enabled Cherokees to become literate after only a few days' study. Very quickly, they established a mail system with distant Cherokees.

established asylums created places where runaway slaves would be safe and secure.

barnacles smallpox.

buffalo men men with wiry hair; Negroes.

Part One
Chapter 11

Summary

Even as Paul D finds himself falling in love with Sethe, he feels inexplicably compelled to distance himself from her. Without knowing why, he stops sleeping in Sethe's bed—moving first to a rocking chair for a few nights, then to Baby Suggs's double bed, and then to the storeroom. Finally, he stops sleeping in the house completely and creates a meager nest for himself in the cold house behind the main house. During this time, he and Sethe continue to have sex and maintain their deepening relationship. However, Paul D believes that Beloved is somehow preventing him from being able to sleep in Sethe's bed. One autumn night, Beloved seeks him out and demands that he "touch [her] on the inside part and call me my name." Although she promises to leave after he repeats her name, she instead forces herself on him.

Commentary

Character Insight

In this brief but crucial interlude, Morrison reveals the ghost's strength by proving her ability to overpower a reluctant adult male. The biblical allusion to Lot's wife, who instantly stiffens into a column of salt for her sin of disobedience, indicates that Paul D realizes the immorality that he contemplates: coupling with a willful, unstable girl whom Sethe loves "as much as her own daughter." By giving in to temptation, he not only betrays his relationship with Sethe but also dissolves the bond between himself, Sethe, and Denver, whose shadows appeared to link hands on the day of the carnival.

Paul D initially appeared to be a normalizing force in Sethe and Denver's lives. His entrance into their lives signaled the beginning of a healthy relationship for Sethe and the introduction of a father figure for Denver. Paul D exorcised the house of its unnatural ghostly presence, rendering it calm and stable for the first time since Sethe's oldest daughter died. At the carnival, Paul D bridged the gap between Sethe and the townspeople, conversing with them in a friendly, easy-going manner. As he, Sethe, and Denver walked home, their joined shadows seemed to signify that Sethe and Denver had accepted him and the normalcy he offered.

However, Beloved's appearance halted the positive changes Paul D had initiated, and in this chapter, the balance of power in the household shifts. Beloved has grown strong enough to force Paul D from the house, just as he once forced her spirit from the house. She then drains the remaining power he possesses by forcing him to have sex with her, which not only undercuts his relationship with Sethe but also destroys the emotional safeguards he had established to protect himself from further suffering.

Literary Device

Like the mating turtles that Beloved observes in Chapter 9, Paul D is encumbered by his shell. He is so out of touch with his motivations that Beloved deceives him into believing that he chooses to abandon Sethe's bed. His body still demands twice daily sexual release, but his subconscious forces him further from warmth and intimacy to the cold, paper-lined shed. Despite his effort to counter Beloved's appeal by fixing his gaze on the false silver idol of the lard can, he yields to "some womanish need to see the nature of the sin behind him." The extended metaphor of the tobacco tin pictures his heart as freed of corrosion; as he penetrates her body, she pierces the core of his heart. The energy expended in the act obscures his sense of sound and the removal of the tin lid, yet the vocal repetition of his release at discovering his "red heart" awakens Denver and ultimately "Paul D himself."

Glossary

prima donna   a temperamental, vain, or arrogant person.

Lot's wife   in Genesis 19:24–26, the woman who disobeys God, looks back to see the destruction of Sodom and Gomorrah, and is turned into a pillar of salt.

Part One
Chapter 12

Summary

Denver feels content with the intimacy that she shares with her phantom sister. Beloved, however, does not share Denver's contentment and continues to press for some unnamed fulfillment. Sethe questions Beloved about her mother, her relationship with whites, and her clothes, but Beloved provides insubstantial replies: She remembers only the bridge and one white man. Sethe concludes that Beloved must have been locked away by a lecherous white male who abused her.

Denver remains convinced that Beloved is the ghost that once haunted 124, and she conceals from Sethe the fact that Beloved is now Paul D's lover. Denver's daily discourse with Beloved is limited to discussions of their chores, neighbors, and family. By winter, Denver is consumed with the task of holding Beloved's interest. One day, the two girls enter the shed for cider, and the door bangs shut. In the dark, Denver weeps because she fears that Beloved has returned to the other side, leaving Denver with "no self."

Like a spoiled, manipulative toddler, Beloved reappears and smiles at Denver's clutch on her hem. Suddenly, Beloved points, but Denver sees nothing. Beloved curls up, closes her eyes, and rocks. Denver, failing to understand, asks if Beloved is alright. Beloved directs her gaze to the darkness, telling Denver that she will find Beloved's face there. Denver sees nothing.

Commentary

The mystery of Beloved's true nature deepens in this chapter as Sethe and Denver unsuccessfully attempt to determine her origins. Beloved offers only vague responses to questions about her past, stating that she remembers a white man, a bridge, and being taken away from her mother. Such ambiguous information allows Sethe and Denver to project their own perceptions of Beloved's identity onto her. While Sethe believes she is an abused young woman, Denver is certain that Beloved is the reincarnation of her dead sister's ghost. Although Beloved's sudden disappearance and reappearance in the cold house seems to substantiate Denver's belief that Beloved is a supernatural being, Beloved's statements and behavior indicate that perhaps she is something more than just the ghost of one dead child.

The scene between Denver and Beloved in the cold house is essential to understanding the depth of Beloved's character and her influence on the other characters in the novel. First, Morrison has established Denver's fascination with Beloved, showing how Denver has altered her daily routines and even her personality to keep Beloved near her. Part of Denver's strategy in this chapter involves asking Beloved to help her carry a cider jug from the cold house. In the cold house, however, Beloved momentarily disappears and Denver panics, distressed over the loss of the one thing that has given her life meaning.

Notice the setting Morrison uses for this scene and her description of Denver's panic. First, even though it is noon—the brightest part of the day—the interior of the cold house is almost completely dark. The few bits of sunlight that slip through the cracks in the roof and walls are swallowed "like minnows" in the darkness. When Beloved disappears, Denver becomes disoriented and distraught. Morrison describes Denver's reaction as if Denver is drowning: "She feels like an ice cake torn away from the solid surface of the stream, floating on darkness, thick and crashing against the edges of things around it. Breakable meltable and cold." Denver has difficulty breathing through her tears and cannot see anything in the darkness. Finally, she decides to "let the dark swallow her like the minnows of light above." Just as she has given up hope of life, Beloved reappears, smiling at Denver's despair.

With Beloved's reappearance, the description of the cold house subtly changes. The "minnows of light" are now described as "the cracklights above" and "the sunlit cracks." Still smiling, Beloved seems to be trying to tell Denver something about herself. She directs Denver's attention to the cracks of light and then tells her, "I'm like this," as she curls her body up, rocking and moaning. Finally, she points into the darkness at a face Denver cannot see, saying, "Me. It's me." Denver doesn't understand what Beloved is trying to tell her, and without close attention to Morrison's hints in the setting, the reader will not understand Beloved's meaning either.

In this scene, Morrison reveals that Beloved represents more than Sethe's dead child. She also represents the slaves who were brought over in the dark holds of ships; slaves who were faceless and nameless and who disappeared from history soundlessly, just as Beloved disappeared in the darkness of the cold house. Denver's experience of "drowning" simulates the countless drownings of slaves in the Atlantic, and Beloved's depiction of herself rocking and moaning demonstrates her experience in the hold of a ship, huddled in the darkness with only a few cracks of light above. Morrison dedicates this book to "sixty million and more"— the estimated number of blacks who died in slavery. Beloved is their voice and their experience. Consequently, in this scene, Morrison shows us that Beloved is a multifaceted character: She is the ghost of a child, the ghost of the nameless slaves, the ghost of a terrible but inescapable past. Sethe and Denver will have to learn to overcome Beloved's power—the power of the past—before they can create a life for themselves in the future.

Glossary

moss rose   a fleshy annual plant of the purslane family, usually with yellow, pink, or purple flowers.

cracklights   glimmers of sun through the cracks.

Part One
Chapters 13 and 14

Summary

Three weeks into his affair with Beloved, Paul D ponders his servitude under Garner, who allowed so much freedom that the male Sweet Home slaves were deluded into thinking themselves men. After schoolteacher took over the management of Sweet Home, the slaves realized that they had nurtured a false sense of security. Paul D's bitter recriminations return him to the scene of Sixo's death, when Sixo displayed his strength by refusing to cry out while his body roasted over flames.

Fears for his lost sense of self impel Paul D to seek Sethe at Sawyer's restaurant. She smiles with "pleasure and surprise" when she sees him and hurries to finish her work. Paul D tries to prepare her for the revelation that Beloved has overpowered and sapped his strong sense of independence. The look of resignation in Sethe's eyes tells Paul D that she expects him to leave her. Inexplicably, he decides not to confess his relations with Beloved, instead proposing that he and Sethe conceive a child.

Paul D's proposal surprises him with its threefold application: A pregnancy would return him to Sethe, salvage his manhood, and break Beloved's hold on him. Sethe cuddles with him on the way home. Snowflakes fall on the couple, and Paul D talks himself into adopting his own suggestion. Joyously, he hoists Sethe on his back and runs toward home.

As usual, Beloved awaits Sethe's return. Holding out a shawl to her mother, Beloved breaks the romantic spell. Concerned for Beloved's health, Sethe instead wraps her in the shawl. Paul D, angry at being displaced in Sethe's affections, scuffs along behind, "icy cold." Seeing Denver, his other adversary, he thinks, "And whose ally you?"

Sethe settles Paul D's quandary by inviting his return to her bed. Paul D realizes that, with Sethe's help, "he could put up with two crazy girls." Sethe, remembering the demands of a mother's love, questions her ability to cope with a fifth child, and she decides that she must decline the offer of another pregnancy. At the same time, Sethe's mind moves a little closer to accepting that Beloved is the child that she has willed to return from the dead.

In the next scene, as Paul D and Sethe return to the upstairs bed, Denver washes dishes while Beloved sucks her forefinger and whimpers, "Make him go away." With finger and thumb she removes a back tooth and fears that her body will self-destruct. At Denver's urging, Beloved cries, knowing that her security slips away as Paul D and Sethe make love.

Commentary

In Chapter 13, the images of dismemberment that permeate the novel become more prominent and more ominous as Sethe scatters animal bones, skins, heads, and innards outside the restaurant for dogs to eat. Her forces seem equally scattered as she considers the possibilities of Paul D leaving her with another child to raise, Buglar and Howard returning home, and Beloved remaining in her life in place of the infant she killed.

Meanwhile, Paul D contemplates what it means to be a man and compares his sense of powerlessness in 124 with the powerlessness he felt as a slave. In 124, he feels alienated from the intimacy of three women who speak their own code. Sethe even acknowledges to herself that "They were a family somehow and he was not the head of it." When Paul D meets Sethe at her work, he is attempting to regain his sense of manhood and his place in the family by taking control of his situation. If he reveals the secret of his relationship with Beloved, he feels he will break free from Beloved's power over him.

When the opportunity comes to be honest with Sethe, though, he is unable to tell her that he is not man enough to fend off a young woman's advances. Instead he asserts his manhood by declaring that he wants Sethe to have his baby. Getting Sethe pregnant would prove his manhood and would also serve to create his own family. Paul D's attempt to reinstate himself in Sethe's life seems to have worked when she invites him to share her bed. However, despite her affection for Paul D, Sethe is determined to resist his attempts to alter the dynamics of her family.

Sethe ponders how to turn down Paul D's proposal without bruising his already battered ego. With a mother's certainty, she recognizes that her family is complete, that the symbolic breaking of waters she experienced when she first saw Beloved on the stump concluded years of dreaming of her baby girl, who was lopped off just like the felled tree. As though assuring the reader that Sethe controls Paul D's destiny, the chapter closes with his chest rising and falling beneath her hand.

Chapter 14 presents Beloved's response to Sethe's decision to bring Paul D back into the house and into her bed. Beloved, who has manifested enough strength to seduce Paul D, now feels herself losing control of her mother's affections and of her power over Paul D. The easy extraction of her tooth signifies how tenuous her physical presence is and how much she depends upon Sethe's attention for her own survival. As Beloved weeps over images of herself physically falling apart, Sethe and Paul D are joined upstairs in intercourse. This simultaneous union and disunion, coupling and dismembering, pushes the dysfunctional family closer to disaster as the snowy weather packs them into the microcosm of 124 Bluestone Road.

Glossary

even learn reading   Laws forbade owners from teaching their slaves to read.

calves of his youth   Paul D, in the absence of available females, found sexual release in intercourse with calves.

fixing me   putting a hex or magic spell on; conjuring.

slats   The Cincinnati sidewalk is made of wooden planks.

Part One
Chapter 15

Summary

In a flashback, Baby Suggs reveals that her joy at the reunion of Sethe and her children was tempered by concern for Halle. On the twenty-eighth day after he delivered Sethe and her newborn baby to freedom, Stamp Paid, an agent for the Underground Railroad, delivers two buckets of blackberries to Sethe's family and feeds a single berry to Denver. Inspired by Stamp Paid's gift, Baby Suggs and her congregation celebrate by creating a feast for 90 people.

In the midst of the joyous event, ill feelings begin to grow toward Baby Suggs and her family. Neighbors participating in the feast grow envious of Baby Suggs's *manumission* (formal emancipation from slavery), her two-story house, her well, and her relationship with the Bodwins, the local Quaker abolitionists who let her live in 124. The next day, as Stamp Paid replenishes the woodpile, Baby Suggs begins to feel that something is amiss and recalls the loss of her four daughters and three sons. She allows herself to linger over memories of Halle, her eighth child—and her favorite—whom Mr. Garner purchased when he brought Baby Suggs from Carolina to assist his wife with kitchen chores.

As slaves, the three Pauls, Sixo, Halle, and Baby Suggs, who limped as a result of a hip displacement, ran Sweet Home. The sight of Baby Suggs's pain bothered Halle so much that he persuaded Garner to let him hire himself out on Sundays to pay for his mother's freedom. Garner, who usually sheltered his slaves on Sweet Home, agreed to the arrangement. In her 60s, Baby Suggs received her emancipation papers. Before delivering her to the Bodwins in Cincinnati, Mr. Garner revealed that Baby Suggs's bill-of-sale name was Jenny Whitlow.

Baby Suggs marveled at the size of Cincinnati, the number of white citizens and two-story houses, and the prospect of working for money. Set up as cobbler, washwoman, seamstress, and canner for the Bodwins, she moved into her own two-story house, which had belonged to the Bodwins' grandparents.

Commentary

Theme

A major premise of Morrison's text is that benevolent masters often did more harm than good. As demonstrated by Mr. Garner's relationship with his slaves, Sweet Home—the embodiment of Stephen Foster's sentimental song "My Old Kentucky Home"—shielded slaves from the harsh world beyond that property. By playing God and creating an artificial haven, Garner ill-prepared his slaves for the shock of a new master, one disinterested in humanitarianism and concerned primarily with profit.

Another revelation from this and other chapters is that the Garners degraded their slaves by thinking of them as children. To Lillian Garner, the notion of a formal wedding for Sethe brought a patronizing upturn of the lips. To Mr. Garner, Baby Suggs's slave name, her only tie with her first mate in a string of eight, was undignified and also inappropriate for Halle, who was fathered by another slave. Garner devalued Baby Suggs's experiences as wife and mother by claiming that Jenny Whitlow was a more fitting name for a "freed Negro." Baby Suggs, who kept her opinions to herself, realized that the only way she could locate her displaced family was to maintain the name by which they knew her. Wherever they were, they would not recognize her if she were called by a white woman's name like Jenny Whitlow.

Glossary

anointed   put oil on in a ceremony of consecration.

strawberry shrug   a version of "shrub," a dessert made from fruit pulp, sweetening, and crushed ice.

rue   any of a genus of strong-scented shrubs of the rue family, esp. an herb with yellow flowers and bitter-tasting leaves formerly used in medicine; symbolizes regret.

rendered fat   fat from cooked pork, skimmed off and hardened into lard.

laid fires   arranged kindling, splits, and back logs to make a fire.

knocked her down (or up)   mistreated or impregnated her.

stud his boys   use male slaves as breeders.

gone to Glory   died.

Bishop Allen   Richard Allen, founder of the AME church.

fixed on   concentrated on.

Part One
Chapter 16

Summary

In another flashback scene, four white outsiders—"schoolteacher, one nephew, one slave catcher and a sheriff"—ride authoritatively toward 124 Bluestone Road. Alert to the value of slaves captured and returned alive, they survey the family scene.

Baby Suggs fans her face while Stamp Paid chops wood. But Sethe has already seen the white men coming and sprung into action. Too late, the foursome stare at the woodshed where Sethe has murdered Beloved, wounded Buglar and Howard, and threatened to bash Denver's brains. Stamp Paid rescues Denver before Sethe can swing the infant into a plank wall.

Schoolteacher partly blames Sethe's extreme reaction to his presence on the "nephew who'd overbeat her and made her cut and run." Faced with a crazy mother, two injured children, and an infant with no wet nurse, schoolteacher realizes that this brood will not profit Sweet Home. The horrific scene impresses the nephew who took Sethe's breast milk, and he trembles as the sheriff takes charge. Schoolteacher and his companions also conclude that too much "freedom" has reduced these slaves to African savagery.

Before the sheriff places Sethe in custody, Stamp Paid tries to take Beloved's corpse from Sethe's clinging hands and give Denver to her mother. Baby Suggs hurries to aid the wounded boys. Sethe relinquishes Beloved and holds Denver to her blood-stained nipple. Denver swallows milk along with her sister's blood. Sitting up straight in the sheriff's wagon, Sethe is taken away amid the wordless humming of onlookers. A red-haired boy jumps out of an approaching cart and gives Baby Suggs a pair of shoes to repair.

Commentary

Literary
Device

Ominous images hovered in Chapter 15, particularly the prickly bracken that Stamp Paid braved to gather blackberries. But for all their destructive power, like the circlet of thorns that crowned Christ's head, the cruel prickers that pierced Stamp Paid's skin yielded the sweet fruit that he fed to the infant Denver. Bitter and sweet overlapped. Likewise, the fullness of the feast at 124, like the loaves and fishes with which Christ fed his followers and the Last Supper that preceded his crucifixion, foreshadowed the black community's betrayal of Sethe, whose unforeseen violence disturbed their peace.

But while Chapter 15 mixed images of pain and sweetness, Chapter 16 pours out a bitter harvest, a slow-motion montage of slavery's worst fears. Far more threatening than thorns or envious neighbors to Sethe and her family are the galloping "four horsemen," the slave-day version of the Four Horsemen of the Apocalypse, portentous embodiments of famine, war, pestilence, and death. Each white male of the foursome represents an aspect of inhumanity. Schoolteacher, who remains unnamed, preserves a cool detachment about the slaves, whom he studies as breeding stock for Sweet Home. The slave catcher, motivated by profit, recognizes the worth of potential captives who must be guarded from violence to preserve their usability and maintain maximum value. The nephew, himself a victim of physical abuse, learns too late about the seeds of violence that he has sown by his inexplicably perverse sexual abuse of a helpless female slave. The sheriff, perhaps the most pathetic of the four riders, must uphold an unjust law that sanctions the capture and return of runaway slaves. He must act without regard to the human cost of a woman's murder of her own child to spare it the torment of slavery.

Glossary

jelly-jar smile   pretended innocence.

cut and run   to flee.

camphor   a volatile, crystalline ketone with a strong characteristic odor, derived from the wood of the camphor tree or synthetically from pinene: used in medicine as an irritant and stimulant.

the singing would have begun at once   If Sethe had been less proud, her neighbors would have begun the soothing songs they instinctively began to mourn the dead. Instead, they hum but intone no words of blessing or comfort.

Part One
Chapters 17 and 18

Summary

Returning to the present, Stamp Paid offers Paul D proof that Sethe was jailed for murdering Beloved. He shows Paul D Sethe's pencil-drawn portrait in a newspaper clipping that describes the murder. Paul D denies that the mouth of the pictured woman belongs to Sethe. Stamp Paid explains how the murder occurred, noting that Baby Suggs felt the approach of danger. He indicates that because of the revelry the previous night, the party-goers dropped their guard and failed to spot "some new whitefolks with the Look." Paul D continues to reject the truth, even after Stamp Paid reads the article aloud.

Paul D asks Sethe for the truth, and her words mix tender memories with horror. Too distraught to sit, Sethe spins around the kitchen, recalling her insufficient knowledge about babies and nutrition, the painting of the steps that enticed the crawling Beloved, and her attempts to work and simultaneously watch over her children at Sweet Home. Paul D realizes that Sethe killed her child with a handsaw. He accuses Sethe of the crime, and then withdraws from the house. Sethe suspects that she may never see Paul D again.

Commentary

A mother killing her own child is an act that subverts the natural order of the world. A mother is expected to create life, not destroy it. The truth about Beloved's death is finally revealed, and Morrison leads up to the story with images of death and unnatural circumstances. The setting for Stamp Paid's revelation to Paul D is the slaughterhouse, where he and Paul D work with death every day. When looking at the newspaper clipping, Paul D immediately recognizes the implications of Sethe's picture appearing in a white newspaper. News about blacks does not normally appear in white papers unless something terrible enough has occurred to capture the white readers' interest. Just as it is unnatural for the white community to acknowledge any blacks, it is unnatural for a black community made up of ex-slaves not to protect their own from white slave catchers. However, that is what happened on the day Sethe tried to murder her children.

Paul D's resistance to Stamp Paid's revelation about Beloved's murder demonstrates the degree of horror and disbelief such an act creates. As we have seen, Paul D has undergone terrible, dehumanizing experiences which have toughened him and made him nearly impervious to hardship and pain. Morrison reminds us of his toughness when she describes his working conditions at the slaughterhouse. Paul D, we know by now, is not a man who is easily shocked. He is horrified, though, by the nature of Sethe's crime and by her inability to comprehend why her actions were wrong.

In a striking reversal of characterization, Sethe dances frenetically through the kitchen after Paul D shows her the clipping. She pours out confessions of her inability to mother her children—to nourish them and protect them from harm while she worked the fields, from fire while pork was being smoked, from the well, and from the stomp of Red Cora's hoof. Paul D, incapable of asking outright if she murdered her own child, looks at Sethe with unquestioning love—"love you don't have to deserve." The climax of their encounter, and of the novel itself, pours out in simple words: "I did it. I got us all out [from schoolteacher's tyranny]." Sethe, beaten down by slavery and despair, flaunts her pride that she—a woman, a slave, a pregnant female—managed to rescue her family, "Without Halle too." To dramatize her deed, she envisions herself as "deep and wide and when I stretched out my arms all my children could get in between." Sethe celebrates her ability to shelter her family.

The pivotal scene hangs on Sethe's final question, "You know what I mean?" Paul D understands why an ex-slave should "[protect] yourself and [love] small," at least until being free of schoolteacher and men like him. He perceives the risk that Sethe took by opening her heart to "a big love . . . [one] that would split you wide open in Alfred, Georgia." Sethe and Paul D continue to connect through individual horror stories—stories of Paul D suffering life on a chain gang and sleeping in a subterranean coffin, and Sethe not being able to "let [Beloved] nor any of 'em live under schoolteacher."

The epiphany that concludes Book I pours out beyond language, outside of the domain of human communication: "No. No. Nono. Nonono." Within Sethe's psyche, metaphoric hummingbirds pierce her headcloth, their wings drumming into her brain a desperate course of action. Therefore, by the time her pursuer reaches her, the child in her arms has pumped out the last of its blood.

Learning the truth, Paul D finally perceives Sethe as a new and different woman, indefinably separate from the child-woman who had taken Baby Suggs's place at Sweet Home. He lashes out at the "thickness" of Sethe's love, which killed one child and drove two more away. Condemning her for wrongdoing, Paul D erects a barrier between them with a singularly uncharitable observation: "You got two feet, Sethe, not four." Like a beast peering through the forest, she correctly identifies his panic and murmurs, "So long."

Glossary

dead Miami   a large Indian tribe that once populated the Ohio Valley before its lands were stolen and its tribal members shunted to reservations in Kansas and Oklahoma.

fagot   a bundle of sticks, twigs, or branches, esp. for use as fuel.

sassafras   a small eastern North American tree of the laurel family, having an aromatic bark, leaves with usually two or three finger-like lobes, and small, bluish fruits.

comfrey   any of a genus of European plants of the borage family, with rough, hairy leaves and small blue, purplish, or yellow flowers, sometimes used for forage or ornament.

Part Two
Chapter 19

Summary

Stamp Paid, upon learning that Paul D left 124 Bluestone Road on the day that he saw the newspaper clipping, scolds himself for violating Sethe's family's privacy. He thinks over the sequence of events that Baby Suggs's family endured after the "Misery" of Beloved's murder and after the death of Baby Suggs shortly before the end of the Civil War. He recalls that after Baby Suggs's death, neighbors distanced themselves from Sethe, who avoided Beloved's funeral service and stood stonily at the graveside. For six days after Paul D leaves, Stamp Paid tries to knock on Sethe's door but cannot find the courage to do so.

On the other side of the door at 124, Sethe tries to rid herself of anger. She decides to take Denver and Beloved ice skating, but before they go, her thoughts return to jail, the loss of her earrings, and small parcels of food that Baby Suggs handed her through the bars. Sethe remembers that during her leave of absence to attend the baby's funeral, Howard and Buglar refused to come near her. Within three months of being jailed, Sethe gained her freedom. She bartered sex for a gravestone and had the carver inscribe one of the words that she heard Reverend Pike say during the funeral service invocation, "Dearly Beloved." Weighed down by these memories, Sethe trudges to work late for the first time in 16 years.

Stamp Paid, pondering the source of his name and wondering if he owed a debt to Denver and Baby Suggs, discusses Sethe's strange household with Ella, who was one of many black neighbors to snub Sethe after Beloved's murder. Ella suggests that Stamp Paid may find answers to his questions from Paul D, who has been sleeping at the church. Stamp Paid chides Ella for not opening her own home to Paul D in a time of need. He rejects Ella's criticisms of Sethe and acknowledges that his own meddling caused Paul D to leave 124.

As Sethe ends her day's work for Sawyer, she recalls how trusting she was at Sweet Home before Mr. Garner's death, when things changed and slaves had to steal, lie, and deceive in order to endure life. She recalls her humiliation at hearing schoolteacher instruct his nephews to catalogue her human traits and her animal traits. The realization that Buglar and Howard would soon be large enough for schoolteacher to sell disturbed her sleep. Sethe congratulates herself for managing to save her children from slavery.

Commentary

Morrison makes it clear that the victimization of former slaves does not stop with their escape from slave states. Law intervenes in Baby Suggs's life all the way to her burial. She enjoys only a four-week acquaintance with her daughter-in-law and grandchildren before schoolteacher, justified by the Fugitive Slave Law, terrifies Sethe into mayhem. Taking to her bed in search of respite from more worries than she can handle, Baby Suggs absorbs herself in the abstract comfort of color until her death. Sethe's order to "Take her to the Clearing," where she wants Baby Suggs buried, also meets opposition from laws that force mourners to bury the popular matriarch in the cemetery.

The classical theme of *hubris* (exaggerated pride), an essential in Greek tragedy, delineates Sethe as the tragic heroine of this story. Because of her outrageous act of self-sufficiency, her neighbors rescind the sympathy and camaraderie usually extended to ex-slaves, and they exile her in the land of freedom that she risked everything to attain. After Baby Suggs's death, mourners refuse to enter 124 or partake of Sethe's food. As Stamp Paid contemplates the family's fate, he blames himself for acting out of mean-spiritedness and envy. By searching for the "pride [that] goeth before a fall" in Sethe, he discloses that pride in his own heart. Shamed by his uncharitable act, Stamp Paid downgrades his own status from a rescuer of runaway slaves and "Soldier of Christ" to an ignoble meddler.

Another classical theme, harmony, crumbles quickly under the weight of local suspicion, blame, and alienation. Before Beloved's death, the community of ex-slaves shared their miseries in the warmth of Baby Suggs's house and shared spontaneous bursts of revelation and rejoicing in the clearing. These connections fade to nothing as Beloved's ghost replaces the spirit of generosity and acceptance. In place of harmony, Sethe rewards herself with the satisfaction that she succeeded in rescuing her children from whipping, lynching, starvation, and sale. Thus, the theme of endurance takes precedence over harmony. Sethe, content in her efforts, locks out the inharmonious neighborhood that turns its collective back on her.

Skating both literally and symbolically on slippery ice, Sethe and Denver share one skate each while Beloved, treated to a full set, receives the privileges accorded a guest. The scene, unobserved by outsiders, ends with Sethe's unforeseen tears. The girls support her both physically and emotionally as they walk back to the house where Sethe provides them with warm milk. But this milk, symbolically thinned by the family's precarious position on Bluestone Road, requires artificial flavoring.

Glossary

dropsy   edema, or an abnormal accumulation of fluid in cells, tissues, or cavities of the body, resulting in swelling.

Fugitive Bill   The Fugitive Slave Bill, tacked onto the Compromise of 1850, required the return of slaves from free states as just c ompensation of owners. Although contested in *Ableman v. Booth,* on October 16, 1859, the Supreme Court upheld the constitutionality of the unpopular law.

setting-up   night-long watch over a corpse.

pride goeth before a fall   a common compression of Proverbs 16:18, "Pride goeth before destruction, and an haughty spirit before a fall."

things older, but not stronger, than He Himself was   that is, evil.

Spirit willing; flesh weak   As described in Matthew 26: 40–41, Christ, in his agony in Gethsemane, the night when he is betrayed, chastises Peter because the disciples have fallen asleep.

Settlement Fee   Pro-Union Southerners pressed claims for damages after their property, supplies, and animals were confiscated by an army quartermaster or commissary or were destroyed during foraging, pillage, or hostile action, such as artillery shelling or arson. On March 3, 1871, Congress began a process of reimbursement for the loyalists' losses. The legislation was extended on May 11, 1872 to cover similar losses caused by U.S. naval action.

God's Ways and Negro pews   contemplation of God's apparent blessing of white people, who continued to isolate black worshippers in segregated pews, often in the "colored balcony."

skin voting   only white people had the right to vote.

Republicans   political movement led by Abraham Lincoln from third-party status to frontrunner.

Dred Scott (1795–1858)   a Southampton County, Virginia, slave who sued for freedom in 1846. Voting seven to two, the Supreme Court dismissed the case of *Scott v. Sanford* nine years later on the grounds that the Constitution did not guarantee rights to a non-citizen. This pro-slavery decision is thought to have hastened the Civil War. Scott, who was freed by his owner in May 1857, died the following year from tuberculosis.

Sojourner's high-wheeled buggy   Sojourner Truth was the alias of Isabella Baumfree (1797–1883), a slave and abolitionist born in Hurley, New York, who was freed when the state emancipated its slaves in 1827. Impelled by religious fervor, Isabel took the new name to announce her mission. She personally led many runaways to freedom and, despite her illiteracy, addressed rallies and women's rights conventions.

Colored Ladies of Delaware, Ohio   a women's organization dedicated to social and civic activities, such as petitioning the courts to free Sethe from a death sentence.

North Star   Frederick Douglass's abolitionist newspaper, published in Rochester, New York from 1847 to 1863.

live oak   a wide-spreading, evergreen oak native to the southeastern U.S. Because it has tough bark and does not lose its leaves, the live oak often symbolizes resilience.

your eyes   here, stove burners.

white satin coat   a residue of cooked milk.

Licking River   a river that branches south from the Ohio River into northern Kentucky.

get right   make amends, apologize, or atone for a personal injury.

in chambers   in private.

you way off the track with that wagon   a common adage meaning "you're overstepping the bounds of courtesy."

you in deep water   You've gone too far.

I'm on dry land   I have just cause.

people who die bad don't stay in the ground   a belief that victims of murder or wrongful death wander the earth as ghosts.

head cheese   a loaf of jellied, seasoned meat, made from parts of the heads and feet of hogs.

measuring string   the tape measure that schoolteacher uses to study black bodies. According to the pseudo-sciences of phrenology and physiognomy, which were popular in the mid-1800s, the shape of the head and body revealed human character, intelligence, and capabilities.

Diane   *dianthus*, any of a genus of plants of the pink family, including the carnation and sweet william.

he had company in the prettiest trees you ever saw   Paul A is hanging from one of the trees of Sweet Home farm.

Part Two
Chapters 20 and 21

Summary

Chapter 20 finds Sethe continuing to wander the past, resolved in her choice to reclaim Beloved. She recalls that she reported to Mrs. Garner that schoolteacher's nephews attacked her while he watched. Mrs. Garner, reduced to invalidism, did nothing about the atrocity. Through the dying woman's bedroom window, Sethe heard shots. Quickly, she entrusted her three children to the woman in the wagon, and Sethe returned to Sweet Home to try to find Halle. The beating she received for freeing her children cost her a piece of tongue, which she bit off when the lash opened the skin on her back.

In Chapter 21, Denver ponders her brothers' fear of their mother after she tried to kill them. Denver admits to herself that she is a recluse: "Not since Miss Lady Jones' house have I left 124 by myself. Never." Her only forays into the world outside 124 have been a burial and the outing to the carnival. Her mind churning from worry that Sethe will harm her and Beloved, Denver remains alert. She frets, "This time I have to keep my mother away from her." She exults that Paul D is gone and vows to hang on "till my daddy gets here to help me watch out for Ma'am and anything come in the yard." The bright spot in Denver's reality is Baby Suggs, who taught her to appreciate and love her own body. The hope of Denver's future is Beloved, who returned to fill the emptiness left by Baby Suggs's death.

Commentary

Sethe contemplates the paradox of Beloved's death. In her musings, Sethe declares that "if I hadn't killed her she would have died and that is something I could not bear to happen to her." A mixture of motherhood images roils in Sethe's tangled internal monologue. She recalls Nan nursing her with the milk left over from the "whitebabies." She thinks about herself tenderly caring for Mrs. Garner during her bout with a grotesque throat tumor. She also contemplates her marriage to Halle.

In one of her frequent, minor epiphanies, Sethe praises herself for what she has accomplished. "I lasted," she boasts, "And my girl come home."

Sethe displays unusual rebellion for an ex-slave as she takes stock of what her choices have brought her. Late to work for the first time in 16 years, she testily rebukes her boss Sawyer, risking the loss of a job with one of the few people willing to hire an ex-con. For the first time, she comprehends Baby Suggs's preoccupation with color and realizes that the freedom to contemplate "what the sun is doing to the day" is a benchmark in an ex-slave's life. Sethe remarks that she also understands why Baby Suggs didn't want "to get to red"—the color that covered Sethe's dying baby.

As Sethe looks to the future, she hopes for a reunion with her "ma'am" and the rest of her family. The memories of her mother's peculiar smile convince Sethe that a steel bit forced her mother's mouth into a semblance of an upturn, like the forced welcome of "Saturday girls" working the slaughterhouse yard. Sethe recalls how close she came to prostitution and that same forced smile, until the Bodwins found her a job that allowed her to earn $3.40 a week to feed her family.

Chapter 21, a companion piece to Sethe's internal monologue in Chapter 20, shifts point of view to the intense needs and insecurities of Denver. Like Sethe, Denver—controlled by the past and a victim of persistent nightmares where "she cut my head off every night"—examines her seclusion, which is made bearable now by the company of her ghostly sister. She recalls the advice of her brothers about how to avoid execution if danger should again force Sethe to desperate parricide. Unpleasant memories float up from Denver's childhood: the sound of scratching, the sight of the dark shed, the smell of desperation emanating from Sethe's dress, and "something little" watching from the corners.

Serving a self-imposed sentence of nameless fear, alienation, and yearning, Denver retreats to "the secret house," the green chapel that shuts out the hurt. In the sheltering clearing, she envelopes her bruised psyche in Baby Suggs's lore: the joy of being alive and free, the pride in being mistress of her own home, and the admiration of Halle, who worked so hard to free his mother from slavery and alleviate her pain. Denver believes that nursing from a breast anointed with Beloved's blood made her immune to the ghost's menace. Isolated and longing for sisterly communion, Denver loves this visitor: "She's mine, Beloved. She's mine."

Part Two
Chapters 22 and 23

Summary

Beloved, a combination of adult body and infant perceptions, tries to describe her experience on the other side, where death is a "dead man on my face" and "daylight comes through the cracks." The strongest emotion left to her is love for Sethe, whom she observes "chewing and swallowing." Intent on eluding a return to the other side, the spirit emphasizes, "I am not dead—I am not."

Commentary

Style & Language

The complements to Chapters 20 and 21 are these two lyric statements by Beloved, whose sensibilities and speech revert to babyhood, thus denying her the logic and expression appropriate to her adult body. As she explains, "how can I say things that are pictures." On "the little hill of dead people," she is troubled by "a hot thing"; the sensory impression Beloved describes represents Sethe's determined spirit, which wills her daughter back to earth. Still impelled by the bond to motherly love, Beloved insists, "I cannot lose her again." The horror of decay and of merging with the elements blends with Beloved's alienation. She mourns, "there is no one to want me——to say me my name." Morrison employs nonstandard spacing and syntax to probe the mind of the dead child: "again again——night day——night day——I am waiting——no iron circle is around my neck." So strong is Beloved's identification with her mother that the child's spirit loses itself in love: "[S]he is the laugh——I am the laugher——I see her face which is mine."

In a surreal depiction of the watery division between earth and the afterlife that fails to separate Sethe from her daughter, the departed spirit remains "in the water under the bridge." Analysts read into this chapter a scene resurrected from the collective unconscious, a murky race memory of the black *diaspora*—the scattering of Africans by ship to slave ports in the New World. Although Beloved had no knowledge of the fearful passage, her oneness with the dead forces her to experience the tight compression of black bodies in the hold of the slaves' galley.

The ghoulish interrogation between mother and murdered child gets at the truth. "Didn't you come from the other side?" Sethe asks. "Do you forgive me? Will you stay? You safe here now." Beloved questions her about "the men without skin," the white men who tried to take her back to Kentucky. Sethe extends the strongest of benedictions—a smile that assures Beloved of safety, blessing, and acceptance.

Chapter 23, a trio for three female voices, harmonizes the strains of Sethe, Denver, and Beloved, each craving and each finding nourishment in love, security, and banishment of the past. The dialogue shifts to Denver, who warns Beloved not to risk too much by loving too much. Vulnerable since the day Stamp Paid rescued her from a violent death against the shed's plank wall, Denver knows that "she can give you dreams." Like some devouring monster, the Sethe whom Denver calls mother "chews and swallows." The only safety is found in another dream, the fantasy of the deliverer: "Daddy is coming for us. A hot thing."

Style & Language

The trio—Sethe, Beloved, and Denver—merge in the final lines, blessed by milk, smiles, and blood. The benediction, like a voodoo incantation, like a classic admirer's charm, is uttered three times, once for each:

You are mine

You are mine

You are mine.

Part Two
Chapter 24

Summary

At the entrance to the Church of the Holy Redeemer, Paul D sips from a liquor bottle and contemplates the crusty exterior that once protected his heart from vulnerability. He relives the demise of Sweet Home, the slave haven that crumbled rapidly after Garner's death. Because Paul D and the other slaves refused to believe Sixo's description of slavery in the outside world, Paul D found the truth the hard way—in the brutal Alfred, Georgia prison camp. The day the male slaves tried to escape from Sweet Home, Sixo was supposed to meet his lover, the Thirty-Mile Woman, and Halle was supposed to bring along his wife and three children. The black female Underground Railroad agent, hidden in the corn, promised to remain a night and half a day and to "rattle" to identify her whereabouts.

Paul D recalls hearing unidentified gunshots that night and seeing Halle inexplicably eat butter from the churn. Sixo joined Paul D and the Thirty-Mile Woman but could not account for the absence of Paul A, Halle, or Halle's family. As schoolteacher, four adults, and some pupils approached the dry creek bed, Sixo pushed his woman out of range. He and Paul D were apprehended. Sixo fought back. Schoolteacher struggled to take him alive but eventually determined that Sixo was of no use to Sweet Home. Schoolteacher lit a fire and roasted Sixo, who was tied at the waist to a tree. Schoolteacher then shot Sixo to quiet his singing to his unborn child, "Seven-O! Seven-O!"

Schoolteacher indicated that he would sell Paul D for $900 and replace him with two young male slaves so that "Sweet Home would be worth the trouble it was causing him." To restrain Paul D, schoolteacher applied the "three-spoke collar." Paul D was hobbling toward a pot of cooked meal when Sethe found him to inquire what had gone wrong. Paul D, shamed by his powerlessness, realized that Sethe was still determined to escape.

Putting together clues from the failed 1855 escape, Paul D deduces that Sethe was assaulted by schoolteacher's nephews shortly after leaving him. Sethe then informed Mrs. Garner of the violation and survived a lashing with "the cowhide." He admires her courage and recognizes that "her price was greater than his; property that reproduced itself without cost." He recalls that he laughed with "the bit in his mouth" as he was hitched to a buckboard bound for the prison camp in Alfred, Georgia. In retrospect, Paul D wishes that he had joined Sixo in his juba song, a celebration of the new life carried by the Thirty-Mile Woman. Humiliated by the dollar figure denoting his worth, by Sethe's greater worth as a breeder, and by Mister, the condescending rooster, Paul D could not guess the degradation that he would endure in the Georgia prison.

Commentary

Character Insight

Paul D endures the sweet noose of love for Halle's former wife, the only woman he has allowed close enough to touch his atrophied emotions. In her house, he becomes "a rag doll"; without her, he probes "what-if thoughts that cut deep but struck nothing solid a man could hold on to." The stark reality of his helplessness is made clear through details—his lack of material goods such as shoes for the journey and his overwhelming ignorance of geography, road signs, and interaction with a free populace.

Although Sethe and Paul D are both dehumanized during their slave experiences, their responses to the experience differ due to their different roles. Sethe derives strength and resolve from her role as a mother. To Sethe, the threat of losing her sons to the auction block and the very real loss of sustenance for her breastfed baby are enough to send her fleeing Sweet Home, despite her heavy belly, her separation from her husband, and the trauma of a severe lashing. Meanwhile, the only role Paul D knows is that of being a man. For Paul D, slavery's devaluation of his personhood equals emasculation. The three-pointed collar shames him in front of Sethe, a woman whose acceptance he obviously values. Paul D flees Sethe's strength and determination after he learns that she murdered a child to spare it a similar life of subjugation. In stereotypical convention of male behaviors, Paul D soothes his wounded ego with liquor, a perverse communion ironically celebrated while seated on the front steps of the Redeemer's church, which is too cold to afford him comfort.

Glossary

dry-goods church   formerly a general merchandise store.

trace   a beaten path or trail left by the repeated passage of persons, vehicles, etc.

Hush, hush. Somebody's calling my name. O my Lord, O my Lord, what shall I do?   lyrics of a familiar spiritual used as a coded message. Such verses form a meaningful segment of black lore, particularly "Follow the Drinking Gourd," the lyrical reminder for runaways to aim for the Big Dipper, or Ursa Major, the constellation that pointed north toward the free states and Canada.

hominy   dry corn (maize) with the hull and germ removed and often coarsely ground (hominy grits); it is boiled for food.

juba   a Southern plantation black dance of the nineteenth century, characterized by a lively rhythm marked by clapping the hands.

Part Two
Chapter 25

Summary

Stamp Paid, still faithful to his Christian calling, finds Paul D at the church, begs his pardon for interfering, and offers him shelter in any home in the black neighborhood. Paul D relieves Stamp Paid's anguish by admitting that Reverend Pike did open his residence to him. Paul D refused the offer because he preferred to be alone. Stamp Paid insists that his black neighbors are hospitable, even if they do react harshly to excesses of pride.

Trying to make amends for interfering with Paul D and Sethe's relationship, Stamp Paid tells Paul D about the anger that caused him to consider killing his wife, Vashti, for her months-long sexual relationship with her white owner. The humiliation he felt from his wife's relationship caused him to change his name from Joshua to Stamp Paid. He states that his desire to murder was as low as slavery ever made him.

As Paul D presses for information about Judy, a black neighbor who has offered to open her home to him, Stamp Paid interrupts with an eyewitness account of Sethe's infanticide. He declares, "She ain't crazy. She love those children. She was trying to outhurt the hurter." Stamp Paid presses Paul D about what he fears in 124. Paul D acknowledges that Beloved's abrupt appearance and behavior disturb him. His rapid calculation of a lifetime of suffering leaves him with one question, "How much is a nigger supposed to take?"

Commentary

The communication between Stamp Paid and Paul D reveals that they both continue to struggle with the emotional upheaval caused by slavery. We've seen how Paul D is haunted by his slave experience, and here Stamp Paid shares the pain of the demoralizing humiliation of his wife's sexual enslavement to a white master who adorned her with a cameo and ribbon. Just as Paul D is unable to accept Sethe's murder of her daughter, Stamp Paid describes how he could not forgive his wife for her relationship with their white master. Additionally, like Paul D, Stamp Paid escaped slavery through a long journey. With a symbolic name and the determination to break for the North, he walked out of slavery and headed toward Memphis and ultimately Cumberland.

When Paul D questions the reason for human suffering and the extent to which a man must bear the burden, Stamp Paid, the stoic sage, remarks that humanity must suffer all it can tolerate.

Glossary

I'm a take   I'm going to take.

Part Three
Chapter 26

Summary

The war of wills continues at 124 Bluestone Road. Beloved, whose belly expands while Sethe starves, becomes Sethe's sole focus after she spots the scar on "the kootchy-kootchy-coo place under her chin"—the scar left by the handsaw. Obsessed with Beloved, Sethe loses her job because Sawyer can no longer depend on her. As demented as Baby Suggs was at the end of her life, Sethe spends her remaining $38 on extravagances, including "ribbon and dress goods. . . . Bright clothes— with blue stripes and sassy prints." The family members eye each other warily. Denver fears for Beloved's life, Beloved demands constant attention and coddling, and Sethe searches for absolution for killing her baby girl. At length, Sethe unloads the hurt of the past, and Beloved accuses her of abandonment. Sethe counters with her hopes that the family can reunite "on the other side, forever."

Accusations and counter-accusations continue. Denver fears that Beloved may stab Sethe in retaliation for leaving her. Sethe and Denver grow faint with hunger and weary from emotional conflict. Denver, encouraged by her grandmother's example and wisdom, goes to her former teacher, Lady Jones, for help. Rejecting charity, Denver insists on working. Through Lady Jones, Denver taps into the generosity of the neighborhood women, who supply food regularly to the starving trio.

Denver's home life deteriorates further as Beloved continues to fatten and falls into despair, screaming "Rain! Rain!" and clawing her throat. Sethe recedes further from sanity as Beloved avenges her murder. Meanwhile, Denver serves her mother and sister as cook, laundress, and nurse. At Nelson Lord's suggestion, Denver seeks work in the Bodwin household.

Denver confesses to Janey Wagon, the Bodwins' servant, the truth about what's happening at 124—her mother's madness, the visiting "cousin," and her own need for a job. Janey deduces that the cousin is a ghost and spreads this news to the community. At 3 p.m. on the Friday when Denver is to assume the role of night nurse to the aging

Bodwins, 30 women approach 124 as Denver awaits Edward Bodwin's arrival. The women pray and begin singing at the edge of the yard as the unsuspecting Bodwin drives up in his cart.

Sethe is chipping ice with a pick, trying to cool Beloved's head, when Bodwin arrives. Hearing the women singing at the edge of the yard, Sethe and Beloved move to the porch to see what is happening. The sight of Bodwin triggers a flashback in Sethe's mind to the day school-teacher and the other slave catchers came to reclaim her family. Racing toward the cart, Sethe fails to recognize the generous Mr. Bodwin, seeing only a white man with a whip in his hand. The ice pick becomes an extension of her hand and her will to protect Beloved.

Commentary

Throughout the novel, the characters have been emotionally crippled by their pasts. Sethe and Denver especially are disabled by their histories. The mental and spiritual wounds caused by slavery are still fresh and have not been allowed to heal. Sethe cannot overcome her outrage and sense of violation from her Sweet Home experiences, nor can she work through the guilt she feels about her daughter's death. Meanwhile, although Denver has never lived as a slave, she suffers from the ramifications of her mother's experiences. Her development was arrested upon her discovery of Sethe's murder of Beloved and Sethe's attempt to murder Denver. The magnitude of this discovery caused Denver to withdraw from the community and to retreat into the sheltered but unhealthy world of 124.

With Beloved's arrival at 124, Sethe and Denver have been faced with the physical manifestation of the very thing that haunts them and keeps them from moving on with their lives. Beloved embodies not just the spirit of the child Sethe killed but also all of the past pain and suffering from which Sethe and Denver have never been able to escape. Initially they are fascinated by Beloved and what she represents, but in this chapter Morrison demonstrates how destructive centering one's life around the past can be. As Beloved feeds upon their fascination, Sethe and Denver's lives devolve into chaos and then into near-starvation.

Character Insight

Denver's recognition that she needs to "step off the edge of the world" and leave the house to find help signifies the beginning of her movement from the paralyzing world of the past into the freedom of the present. By taking this step, Denver re-enters the black community and propels herself into womanhood. Every connection she makes to other community members draws her farther from her mother and Beloved's unhealthy love and deeper into a life of possibilities. She learns to read, gets a job, and experiences her first feelings of attraction to a man.

Theme

Carrying on the pervasive theme of the lingering trouble caused by slavery, Lady Jones epitomizes the half-breed, "Gray eyes and yellow woolly hair, every strand of which she hated." An altruistic lover of children, she exerts maternal love to vault over her own isolation, widowhood, and failing vision. Recognizing Denver's needs, she envelops the young woman in love. Lady's intuitive assessment of the situation at 124 Bluestone Road leads her to share "rice, four eggs and some tea" with Denver.

Lady Jones's outpouring of charity serves as partial payment for the sufferings that every ex-slave has known in servitude. Morrison describes the pain that assaulted Baby Suggs, Ella, Stamp Paid, and Paul D: "That anybody white could take your whole self for anything that came to mind. Not just work, kill, or maim you, but dirty you. Dirty you so bad you couldn't like yourself anymore. Dirty you so bad you forgot who you were and couldn't think it up."

Denver's initial visit to Lady Jones and her subsequent visits to the other women in the community serve to reestablish the connections between the community and her family. To Janey Wagon, Denver's story is worthy gossip. To some hearers, it is gospel; to others, fiction. To Ella, it seems unlikely that family members could "just up and kill" their own kind. Whatever the people think of the situation at 124, they feel connected enough to the family again to try to help in different ways. While some people simply offer food, others decide they need to exorcise Beloved from the house. This decision represents a long-awaited reversal of their decision to shun Sethe and punish her for her excessive pride.

The final scene of the chapter, in which Sethe tries to kill Edwin Bodwin, seems to be an echo of the scene in which the schoolteacher comes to 124 to reclaim Sethe and her children. However, whereas that event led to the destruction of a family and its place in the community, this situation leads to healing and reintegration. In this scene, members of the community have come to offer help rather than turn away as they did when the slave catcher came for Sethe. Additionally, the white man coming to take Sethe's child this time is coming to help rather than to hurt. Finally, Sethe chooses to destroy the perceived threat here rather than sacrifice Beloved for a second time.

The combination of all these elements leads to Sethe leaving Beloved on the porch and rushing into the crowd of women, followed closely by Denver. Beloved watches Sethe and Denver disappear into the "hill of black people, falling" which is overshadowed by the white man with a whip. This image is obviously one of slavery—the massive number of blacks who have been dominated by the slave master's whip. Sethe and Denver blend into this image; they cannot escape the ramifications of slavery any more than any other African American. However, as we have seen with Denver throughout the chapter, past oppression and suffering do not mean that people cannot build new lives for themselves.

Ironically, Edwin Bodwin, a well-off white gentleman, shares the horror of slavery to the degree that he and fellow Quakers have warred against it. As it did for Paul D, Stamp Paid, Ella, Lady Jones, and Sethe, the inhumanity of the slave era has drawn Bodwin and his associates into the fray. His generosity with the Bodwin family home led to local scandal after Sethe, his tenant, murdered her child. When Sethe was jailed, quick-witted Quakers "managed to turn infanticide and the cry of savagery around, and build a further case for abolishing slavery."

Glossary

new stitches   perhaps, decorative handwork or new clothes.

chippy   a prostitute.

Wilberforce   a black college in Wilberforce, Ohio, named for William Wilberforce (1759–1833), a noted abolitionist who moved the English government to end the slave trade in the British Caribbean.

normal school   a teacher's college.

sweet thorny place was made up of paper scraps containing the handwritten names of others   the symbolic nest at Lady Jones's house where Denver enters the sisterhood of other black women, who are providing ample food and bits of paper containing their identities so that Denver can return food containers to their owners.

a blackboy's mouth full of money   a derogatory knickknack that depicts a black youth on his knees, his mouth spread as wide as a cup to hold loose change.

mouth harp a primitive monotonal metal musical instrument that is held by the lips and vibrated against the teeth.

a hairy white thing Ella's deformed child fathered by her white owner.

Society the Society of Friends or Quakers, prime movers in the abolitionist movement.

Part Three
Chapter 27

Summary

The return of the aged Here Boy signals the end of Beloved's tenure at 124. Some eyewitnesses declare that she "exploded right before their eyes." Paul D returns, first to the shed and then to the house, which Bodwin, at his sister's command, intends to sell. Stamp Paid's retelling of the story of Sethe's attack and Ella's quick-witted halting of a second murder pales beside local curiosity about the mysterious, big-bellied, naked black woman who disappeared from the porch.

While walking to work, Paul D passes Denver as she leaves the Bodwins' house and heads toward the shirt factory to apply for a job. More confident, sophisticated, and mature than Paul D remembers her, Denver is unable to answer questions about Beloved's identity and sidesteps Paul D's surmise. Again inside the door of 124, he confronts a mix of "ribbons, bows, bouquets." Hearing Sethe humming in the keeping room, he finds her gravely disoriented and thinking of the days when she made ink for Sweet Home.

Paul D encourages Sethe to get up and take hold of her life. He challenges her to escape the type of withdrawal that Baby Suggs experienced in her waning days by suggesting a bath and foot massage. He listens to her anguish and recalls her courtesy in ignoring "his neck jewelry—its three wands, like attentive baby rattlers, curving two feet into the air." Sethe preserved his shattered manhood on that last day at Sweet Home, and he returns the favor by rebuilding her self-esteem with affirmation that she is worthy.

Commentary

Literary Device

Linked with water images, Beloved, who dwelled in water beneath the bridge during her tenure in the land of the dead, engulfed Paul D in an ocean wave of possessive emotion. On his return to the shed, he relives the powerlessness of being devoured by "a life hunger" that he could control no more than he could stop his lungs from gulping air.

After the overwhelming passion ended, he realized that their coupling "wasn't even fun." Like a landed fish, he lay "beached and gobbling air," safely returned from "some ocean-deep place he once belonged to." As though reliving a prenatal experience, he views his release from Beloved as a kind of birthing.

The female/water images segue neatly into Paul D's wartime experiences. He perceived the land as a breast and "fingered its earth for food, clung to its banks to lap water and tried not to love it." Toiling first in a Confederate body reclamation squad and then in foundry work, he wandered in Alabama from Selma to Mobile and then took a skiff from Mobile Bay to a Union gunboat, which carried him to Wheeling, West Virginia. On his own, he journeyed to Trenton, New Jersey, and remained seven years before wandering west toward southern Ohio and Sethe.

In contrast to Paul D, Sethe's tie with womanhood pushes her dangerously toward death. Her body is depleted, her will expired, and her maternal breasts—the ones that nourished four children—symbolically exhausted. Paul D—himself wearied, but grateful to be back with his woman—recalls Sixo's definition of love: "The pieces I am, she gather them and give them back to me in all the right order." In a touching role reversal, Paul D takes on the task of massaging Sethe's body and soul. Sethe leans on Paul D and confesses her stunning loss: "She was my best thing." Paul D, the patient, maternal, Christ-like confessor, strikes the fitting chord with his reminder, "You your best thing, Sethe. You are."

Glossary

Oberlin   a coeducational liberal arts college in Oberlin, Ohio, which in 1835 became the first in the nation to integrate.

you sure 'nough knew her   In the biblical sense, Paul D had sexual knowledge of Beloved, who apparently was pregnant with his child.

battlefields of Alabama   The Union army captured the Tennessee Valley in 1862; Montgomery fell to Union troops in 1865.

Part Three
Chapter 28

Summary

Beloved disintegrates into nothingness, thereby opening the way to wholeness for Sethe. Gossips forget her over time. Sethe and Denver gradually heal from their harrowing battle with the tireless, vindictive ghost. The sound of a skirt rustling sometimes reminds the family of Beloved's tenure at 124. Footprints come and go at creek side. Eventually, Beloved, like the wind or spring thaw, is "disremembered and unaccounted for."

Commentary

Morrison, who has carried ghost conventions far past their gothic origins, ends her story with a well-earned and gratifying peace. Some of Beloved's yearnings remain distant, particularly "the underwater face she needed," a reference to her lack of personhood, which was cut off in its formative stage. The neighbors hush their ungentle gossip, and harmony returns to Bluestone Road. Sethe and Denver, no longer imprisoned by the invidious third party, sink into the rhythm of the seasons. The backyard creek, symbolic of time, womanhood, and, by extension, all life, continues to flow. The ghost's footprints recede into nature as Beloved, returned to her grave, no longer clamors for her mother's kiss.

CHARACTER ANALYSES

Sethe 89

Beloved 89

Denver 90

Baby Suggs 91

Paul D. 91

schoolteacher 92

Sethe

An iron-willed, iron-eyed woman, Sethe is haunted not only by the ghost of her dead daughter but also by the memories of her life as a slave. While she has been scarred by the physical brutality of school-teacher's nephews, she seems even more deeply disturbed by her discovery that most white people view her as nothing more than an animal. She asserts her humanity through her determination to reach freedom and to give her children a free life. Her escape from Sweet Home demonstrates the force of her will to overcome impossible circumstances and foreshadows the desperate measures that she'll take to keep her children from becoming slaves.

Much of Sethe's internal struggle also derives from her ambiguous relationship with her mother. Because of the long hours her mother worked, Sethe barely knew her. However, through Nan she knows that she was the product of a loving union. Of all her mother's children, Sethe was the only one given a name and allowed to live. The comfort she may derive from this knowledge is tempered, though, by the suspicion that her mother was trying to run away when she was caught and hanged. If her mother was indeed trying to escape, she was abandoning Sethe in the process. This abandonment was twofold, because her mother not only left Sethe without her only living relative, but she also forced Sethe to face the horrors of slavery on her own.

Her mother's abandonment affected Sethe deeply and helps explain the choices she makes as a mother. Notice Sethe's resolve *not* to do the same thing to her children. She refuses to leave them without a mother when they've gone ahead to Ohio, and she risks her own life to reach them. When faced with the reality that her children may be sent back into slavery, Sethe chooses to free them through death rather than allow them to encounter even a portion of her past experiences. In Sethe's mind, killing her children to save them from slavery is the ultimate expression of a mother's love.

Beloved

Some debate exists over the identity of Beloved. While some critics claim that she is the spirit of Sethe's murdered daughter, others argue that she is a human woman who is mentally unstable. The most common interpretation of the Beloved character, however, is that she is the spirit of Sethe's dead child and, as Denver notes, "something more."

That something more is a collective spirit of all the unnamed slaves who were torn from their homes in Africa and brought to America in the cramped and unsanitary holds of slave ships. You can find evidence for this interpretation in Beloved's stream of consciousness narrative in Chapter 22. In this chapter, Beloved remembers crouching in a hot place where people are crowded together and dying of thirst.

Because Sethe's mother came from Africa, the experience that Beloved remembers is also Sethe's mother's experience. In a sense, Beloved is not only Sethe's daughter but her mother as well. Because Beloved is supernatural and represents the spirit of multiple people, Morrison doesn't develop her character as an individual. Beloved acts as a force rather than as a person, compelling Sethe, Denver, and Paul D to behave in certain ways. Beloved defines herself through Sethe's experiences and actions, and in the beginning, she acts as a somewhat positive force, helping Sethe face the past by repeatedly asking her to tell stories about her life. In the end, however, Beloved's need becomes overwhelming and her attachment to Sethe becomes destructive.

Notice that Morrison dedicates the book to "sixty Million and more," an estimated number of people who died in slavery. Beloved represents Sethe's unnamed child but also the unnamed masses that died and were forgotten. With this book, Morrison states that they are beloved as well.

Denver

Denver experiences the most positive personal growth in *Beloved* and represents the African American hope for the future. Sethe comments that Denver is a charmed child, and indeed Denver seems to survive impossible circumstances. However, physical survival is not enough. Denver displays intelligence and promise as a child, but her innocence is destroyed when she discovers what Sethe did to her sister and planned to do to her as well.

With the loss of her brothers and grandmother, Denver becomes increasingly isolated and self-centered. Even as a young adult, her attitude is still very childlike; for instance, she behaves rudely when Paul D arrives and wants only to hear stories about herself. Denver's initial immaturity demonstrates how Sethe's inability to escape her past has also trapped her daughters. One daughter, Beloved, is dead and remains forever a child haunting their house, and the other daughter, Denver, lives as a child, never venturing beyond her own yard.

Beloved's arrival at 124 marks the beginning of Denver's transformation. She finally has someone to devote herself to—someone to love. Note how Denver becomes industrious after Beloved arrives, whereas before she was lazy. As Beloved gradually takes over the house and weakens Sethe, Denver recognizes that the family's survival rests upon her shoulders. Denver is finally able to step out of Sethe's world into the outside world and begin her own life. By the end of the novel, Denver is a mature young woman who has become a part of a larger community and who appears to have a future of love and family ahead of her.

Baby Suggs

Baby Suggs acts as a mother figure and stabilizing force for Sethe and Denver. A self-proclaimed preacher, Baby Suggs draws upon the beauty of nature to make the community of ex-slaves recognize the beauty in themselves. She provides a nurturing and healing presence for those scarred by slavery, including Sethe.

When the black community betrays her and doesn't warn her or Sethe about the schoolteacher's approach, Baby Suggs loses her faith in people. She withdraws from the community into an internal world of colors and introspection. Her withdrawal allows Sethe to withdraw as well, leading to a long estrangement with the townspeople. Baby Suggs's influence is vital enough, however, that her presence is felt after her death—not in a haunting way like Beloved's spirit, but in a strengthening way in which her words and attitudes linger in the minds of those who loved her. Her presence helps comfort Sethe even years after she dies, and it encourages Denver to leave the house and seek help.

Paul D

A kind and meditative man, Paul D's memories rival Sethe's in their shocking nature. However, whereas Sethe's past continues to dominate her, Paul D has begun to move beyond his past and to envision a future of hope. His entrance into Sethe's life represents the potential for a happier future for her and Denver.

Because he came from her past and shares some of the experiences that haunt her, Sethe can open herself up to Paul D and find some relief in sharing the burden of her memories. Sethe is drawn to the promise of happiness that she finds with Paul D, but Beloved's arrival stops her movement toward what he represents. Intelligent and perceptive,

Paul D recognizes the danger in Beloved's presence but is unable to do anything about it. All he can do is challenge Sethe's vision of herself and her children. In the end, after Beloved leaves, you sense that Paul D will provide a healing force for Sethe, again offering her the possibility of a brighter future and helping her learn to love herself.

schoolteacher

The only purely evil character in the novel, the schoolteacher is frightening for his detached and methodical cruelty. His pursuit of "knowledge" is especially disturbing, because it demonstrates a rationalization for racism that easily leads to a rationalization for murder. His belief that slaves are nothing more than animals brings to mind the dehumanization of Jews during World War II. Like Beloved, the schoolteacher is not a fully developed character. Instead, he is a representation of the evil in human beings that justifies the degradation of other people and supports murder as a solution to social problems.

CRITICAL ESSAYS

Beloved and Its Forerunners 94

Form 95

Settings 98

Themes 100

Motifs 101

Style 103

Women in *Beloved* 104

A Note on Slavery 105

Beloved, the Film 105

Beloved and Its Forerunners

An offshoot of the universal literary tree, Toni Morrison—for all her feminism and her historical, cultural, and social background—shares much with the white male writers who have also delineated journeys of the spirit.

As in Henry James's *Turn of the Screw*, her characters in *Beloved* confront an elusive ghost, which deprives Sethe of the ability to nest and to know contentment.

Sharing an obsession with social injustice with John Steinbeck's *Grapes of Wrath,* Morrison's novel recreates an emotional landscape that moves beyond historic fact to individual suffering. Not unlike Rosasharn Joad, Sethe communicates maternal love through breast milk.

Mirroring the despair of William Styron's *Sophie's Choice, Beloved* details a clinging ambivalence fed on a past so lurid and unrelenting that it will give the suffering mother no respite. In Styron's novel, visions of Sophie's daughter handed over to Nazi child-burners lead to mental disintegration and alienation from love. In Morrison's, Sethe's torment refuses to dissipate, threatening not only her own well-being but that of Denver.

Like Hester Prynne, who is consumed by secret sin and alienation in Nathaniel Hawthorne's *The Scarlet Letter,* Sethe's paralysis and longing alternately confine and impel her toward a new and healing love and ease Denver into a supportive community of women. At the end of *Beloved,* Sethe has withdrawn from the world, much like Hester at the end of *The Scarlet Letter.* However, whereas Hester's isolation is caused by her relationship with Arthur Dimsdale, Sethe's relationship with Paul D appears to be an impetus for her to re-enter society.

William Faulkner's *As I Lay Dying* and *The Sound and the Fury* influence Morrison's preference for circular narrative and the pervasive theme of human bondage, which the surrender at Appomattox failed to obliterate.

James Joyce's "The Dead" and *Ulysses,* composed in enigmatic glimpses of motive and response, influence Morrison's richly evocative narration, set with jewels of dialogue and conscious thought, both of which lead the characters through a hell of learning how to grasp happiness and security.

Critics find strands of other influential themes and stylistic mannerisms in *Beloved,* notably the insupportable corruption that demands retribution in Joseph Conrad's *Heart of Darkness;* the burden of the desperate act and its equally desperate denouement in E.L. Doctorow's *Ragtime;* the consuming guilt of Herman Melville's *Benito Cereno;* Charles Dickens's symbolic character names; Alice Walker's submergence in the yearnings of motherhood in *The Color Purple;* the lovingly supportive alliance of one black and one white in Mark Twain's *Huckleberry Finn;* and the dark reflection on hard scrabble community life, which generates uncharitable rivalry between haves and have-nots, as delineated in Richard Wright's *Black Boy* and *Native Son.*

Obviously, Toni Morrison is well schooled in literature, yet the urgency and pathos of her characters and situations are uniquely her own.

Form

Beloved, a sophisticated and powerfully evocative stream-of-consciousness novel, seems at once as old as Homer, as terrifying as *Jane Eyre* and *Wuthering Heights,* as philosophical as the *Meditations* of Marcus Aurelius, and as familiar as the Bible. Without becoming tedious or pedantic, Morrison blends a number of traditions:

- the **journey,** which takes Sethe from Sweet Home to Baby Suggs's home, across the river from Kentucky on the southern rim of Ohio. The physical journey, made arduous by a mutilated back, swollen feet, and a premature infant, hardly compares with the spiritual journey, which introduces Sethe to freedom and the most precious reward of all, a real family life. In stereotypically male fashion, Paul D follows his own route and, by deliberate indirectness, arrives at the same point. Reunited with Sethe, he is at last able to surrender himself to the nurturing role that Baby Suggs enjoined her followers to embrace—to love the body, to honor self.

- **coming-of-age,** which allies Sethe's realization of adult powers with a similar growth in Denver. Like successive ocean waves, Baby Suggs wearies of life, leaving the household to Sethe, who in turn crumbles, takes to her bed, and abdicates authority to Denver. Stunted by slavery, each of the women travels the unfamiliar path with imperfect directions. Baby Suggs was wrenched from Africa and forced aboard a slave ship. Sethe was likewise wrenched from her mother and handed into the maimed arms of a wet nurse. Denver, the next in the chain of female victims, lacks security and self-esteem but knows instinctively that the beguiling phantom is the sister for whom she has yearned. The longings of the three women, echoed by Lady Jones, Ella, Janey Wagon, and Patsy, expand coming-of-age into a coming-of-era, when human beings of both sexes can grasp their rightful heritage of personhood.

■ the theme of **grace**, the blessings that don't have to be earned but which, like Christ's beatitudes in the Sermon on the Mount, pour out from charitable hearts touched by sufferings common to the human condition. Each figure in the Bluestone cast carries its burden of hurt, humiliation, and shame. Each, for whatever reason, responds to the complex social milieu at slavery's end by offering small gifts. One helps bind Sethe's tortured body, another weeps into the cooking pots, and a third tends the baby. A series of givers leaves humble packets of food marked by signed scraps of paper. Like shepherds presenting lambs to the Christ Child, the good-hearted black community shares its meager stores.

■ the **symbolic healing caress,** a convention that recalls the tradition of medieval kings who placed a ritual touch on the sick. The touch of blessing permeates the story—from Amy's gentle massage and makeshift bandage for Sethe's feet to Baby Suggs's compassionate, methodical washing of Sethe's body, quadrant by quadrant; from Paul D's blessing of Sethe's hideous tree-like scar to his loving return to Sethe's bedside to anoint her feet and accept her for the powerful woman she once was and still can be. The motif grows more focused on womanhood through the use of myriad breast images, which connect suckling with the maternal will to raise healthy, whole, and safe babies, whatever the cost. By extension, Baby Suggs offers a spiritual caress to the worshippers who surround her miniature Sermon on the Mount in the clearing. Her message restores their sense of self-worth by urging them to love their physical bodies, which have been so discounted by slavery that, like Paul D, they have confronted themselves in terms of dollar value.

- the **symbolic role of nature,** which forms a sheltering chancel over Denver and reconnects her with Baby Suggs, the stable "parent" whose passing left Denver no anchor in rough seas. Water images, psychologically and rhetorically projecting life and motherhood, form a wavy, indistinct cover over Beloved's interment. The terrifying hot/cold, clear/murky figures express the ghost-child's great yearning to reunite with her mother and to complete the growth process cut short by a stroke of a handsaw. The suggestion that Beloved experienced the wretched sea voyage bearing slaves from Africa to America links all blacks with a trial by water, an unholy baptism for aborted infants, a watery grave for those who expired along the way. Beloved's mission is ended by the redeeming love of women, who intervene in Sethe's demented attack on yet another white buggy driver. Beloved, bulging with the unborn child begotten in the same shed where she was sacrificed, fades from sight, then resurfaces in wispy gossip, sightings, and footprints along the creek. But the recovery at 124 Bluestone signals Beloved's return passage over the bridge to her final rest, far from earth's troubled people.

- the **red heart,** an emblem of love, passion, and religiosity, recalls the typically Catholic pictures of Christ exposing his suffering heart. To Paul D, entering Sethe's house and being greeted by a "pool of red and undulating light," the pulsating welcome offers shelter that he accepts at great risk to his manhood. Later, his emotions, crumbled like moldering tobacco in a rusty tin, must rediscover unconditional love and know it for its mixed blessing. Ultimately, he rejects the temporary solace of liquor and a cold church basement to sort out his emotions and define a place for himself among the women of 124 Bluestone. Ironically, the redeeming heart that exonerates and rejuvenates Sethe is Paul D's.

- the traditional triad of **philos, eros,** and **agape,** the Greek names for belonging, passion, and charity, describe the levels of belonging that ex-slaves embrace upon landing on free turf. Having crossed the water from the bloody side to a non-slave state, Sethe passes through the stages of welcome and acceptance as a community member, mother, daughter-in-law, and lover. She loosens her bonds to Halle by inviting Paul D to share her bed. The triad proves fragile, however, after the ghost imposes itself between *eros* and *agape*. Beloved seduces Paul D; Stamp Paid weakens Paul D's bond with Sethe by revealing her murderous past. Ultimately, *philos* triumphs as the community forces Sethe back from violence and embraces her once more as a sister. Then the triad can reform—this time, firm in its balance. Sethe, absolved of her frenzied infanticide, can leave her bed, love her man, accept her grown girl, and walk with pride and camaraderie among her neighbors down Bluestone Road.

Settings

Through circular narrative, "rememory," and oral history, Morrison's characters play out their mutual hurt in a wide array of settings, from a Georgia prison camp to a Cherokee village, from an idyllic Kentucky plantation to the banks of the Ohio River.

For Sethe, birth occurs somewhere on a southern plantation, where her unnamed mother bends into the watery fields among a host of maternal ma'ams and slaves who dance the antelope. Maturity nets Sethe separation and resettlement in Kentucky, where she works in a white woman's kitchen and nightly rests atop a mattress on her cabin's dirt floor. Sweet Home, haunted by a "headless bride" and young men lynched in its luxuriant trees (one of which is named Brother), has its own peculiar beauty that is captured in nature, especially the small cornfield where Halle couples with Sethe, making the stalks wave, flaunting the lovers' private first-time tryst. In the one spot Halle expected togetherness, the wrecked rows of new corn evolve into the ruptured maidenhead edged with youthful pubic hair. Morrison, developing the image with lavish grace, stresses the youth of an enslaved virgin still clad in silk that is "fine and loose and free."

Eighteen years later, the scene shifts to 124 Bluestone Road and a spiteful, gray and white two-storied house with shed, keeping room, storeroom, privy, cold house, and porch. Limited in its outreach, it has only one door, through which journeying blacks pass from way station back to the plank road, which leads them on a perplexing odyssey toward scattered loved ones. The front of the lot sweeps past a field and circular boxwoods into the glade as though the house, unprotected from Beloved's spite, must fend for itself in the open.

In Cincinnati, far from the misshapen Mrs. Garner, the atavistic savagery of the "mossy teeth," and schoolteacher's sadism, Sethe sinks into the masochism of a fruitless emotional duel with her dead child's ghost. These emotional battles are virulent enough to rock the house on its foundations, smashing glass and rending a table leg. Only the steadying male hand of Paul D forces Beloved to abate her attacks and leave Sethe temporarily in peace.

To relieve the tension of this tight camera angle on a single house wracked by three warring females, Morrison selects an oddly evocative mix of side journeys. When Paul D chooses to make a public statement of his intentions, he leads his two women to the carnival, which is set alongside a lumberyard decked with late season roses reeking of over-ripe perfume. The freaks of the sideshow contrast the hand-holding shadow that predicts a family threesome.

In later scenes, after Beloved derails Sethe's small increment of security, Morrison reveals glimpses of Cincinnati's coldly judgmental black community. Paul D, whom Stamp Paid locates on the steps of the Church of the Holy Redeemer, sits in sunshine and indulges in strong drink from a bottle decked with a golden chariot. Along the plank road, a rider approaches, spurring Stamp Paid into the elaborate know-nothing guise of the Negro who has no information to share with the white outsider.

The women, too, briefly desert the too-confining walls of 124 to skate in private on slippery ice, a heavily symbolic bit of escapism that brings them a snatch of joy. Their adventure concludes with a kitchen communion scene graced with warm milk. More hospitable than the cold comfort of Sawyer's restaurant and vastly more inviting than the slaughterhouse where prostitutes smile in desperation and copulate standing up against rough-hewn walls, Sethe's house, for all its dismal past, is a real home. Its welcome draws Paul D upstairs, but the quarrelsome female trio, led by the bumptious ghost, eventually forces Paul D to the shed and Denver to dreamy, post-adolescent withdrawal in the boxwood circle out back.

Later, as Denver approaches desperation, she returns to Lady Jones's husbandless house, where the "post and scrap-lumber fence was gray now, not white" and the stone porch sits "in a skirt of ivy pale yellow curtains at the window." From her former teacher's welcoming abode, Denver moves on to guaranteed work at the Bodwins' house, lush with carpet "thick, soft and blue. Glass cases crammed full of glistening things. Books on tables and shelves. Pearl-white lamps with shiny metal bottoms. And a smell like the cologne she poured in the emerald house, only better." The jewel-like interior, itself only a way station for black sojourners, plays false with Denver and her hopes of renewal because of its statuette—a subservient black holding coins in his mouth—and its owners' hopes of molding her into a student at Oberlin. With more maturity than she has mustered in past episodes, she departs, bound for a job at the shirt factory, support for her ailing mother, and self-actualization.

Themes

Predominant among Morrison's themes is the presence of evil. The ghost of Beloved—an ironic name that might have had "Dearly" carved ahead of it on the tombstone if Sethe had allowed herself ten more minutes with the gravestone carver—makes itself felt in "turned-over slop jars, smacks on the behind, and gusts of sour air." Later, like a flesh-and-blood poltergeist, Beloved rests under a tree on the Thursday that Paul D, Sethe, and Denver return from the carnival. Shortly after, she creates unsubtle havoc by alienating Paul D from the two women he has begun to think of as family. However, like the table standing on three good legs and a reasonably stable repaired leg, the family, on the surface, appears strong enough to support daily demands.

In Morrison's own terms, the controlling theme of the novel is "how women negotiate or mediate between their nurturing compulsion to love the other, the thing that's bigger or better than they are in their lives—husband, children, work—and the other part, which is the individual separate self that has separate obligations." As Sethe confronts evil in herself and in the institution of slavery, motherhood itself rescues her from the oblivion of guilt, shame, and madness. Without the underloved ghost or the coddled, sheltered Denver, Sethe might have disintegrated from within, pulled apart by her "rememory." Instead, she takes refuge in love for her children, and she tentatively, excitedly acknowledges the ego that Paul D returns to nurture—"Me? Me?"

The struggle to love in an inhuman system that breeds children like suckling pigs results in inhuman choices. For women like Sethe's ma'am, some children must be discarded, flung overboard or crudely aborted. For women like Ella, nature mercifully quenches the light within the "white hairy thing," the freakish offspring of a monstrous multiple sexual assault. For Baby Suggs, slavery itself gobbles up offspring, selling some and chasing others with dogs and lashes. The unsuckled breasts of the slave women forced back into rice or indigo fields symbolize the unfulfilled maternity that withers, leaving the deep yearning that empowers Sethe to survive flogging and mammary rape and to flee toward the spiritual all-mother who encourages her to find the grace to love herself.

Another significant theme within *Beloved* is that of history. The main characters of the novel are haunted by their personal histories and by the history of their people. The character of Beloved may represent the physical manifestation of history, signifying how the past can invade the present. As Sethe nearly loses her identity and life through her obsession with her past and her resurrected daughter, Morrison demonstrates how focusing on the past can be all-consuming and destructive. Ultimately, Sethe begins to regain her life by discovering that she has a future. Paul D tells her, "Sethe . . . me and you, we got more yesterday than anybody. We need some kind of tomorrow." Through the healing love of Paul D, Denver, and the black community, Sethe can learn to let go of the terrible history that has defined her. She may discover that she can define herself through the future she creates with her family.

Motifs

Water images abound, such as Nan pointing out to Sethe her mother wading in the flooded indigo field, the convicts' escape during the flood, and the flow of amniotic fluid from Sethe's womb as the infant Denver forces her way into the light. The shape of the canoe, an oversized replica of the female vulva, emphasizes the importance of the birth of the one child that Sethe intends to hang on to. After Beloved's water-soaked wade from the Ohio River shore, Sethe experiences a recurrence of flooding waters, this time from an incontinent bladder inordinately full of urine. Beloved, croupy and thirsting, gulps four cups of water, and then sleeps for four days and wets the sheets, which Denver rinses in secret. Upon Paul D's arrival at 124 Bluestone Road, he detects the female "shining" on Sethe's bare legs, the same symbolic seminal fluid she wiped from her skin the day that she accepted Halle from among the five lustful brothers at Sweet Home.

Temporarily, water freezes into ice firm enough to hold the three women, sliding on one whole pair of skates and one shared pair. Like their tenuous family triad, the happy scene results in slips and mishaps, and then crumbles into unforeseen tears from Sethe. Her solution is the liquid of life, the warm milk that they drink to warm themselves, just as they did in babyhood when Sethe held her breast to their thirsting lips.

Breast and milk images are frequent as well. The first is a reminder of the maternal role of Ma'am, Sethe's mother, who discards unnamed offspring resulting from inappropriate matings and then burns the tender flesh under her breast with circle and cross, as though embracing with the circle and delineating with the cross the child she intended to nurture. This image prefigures the viciousness of Sethe's assault in the barn. Rather than the tearing of her flesh, Sethe recalls the deprivation of nourishment for her infant.

After Paul D reveals to Sethe that Halle witnessed her attack and smeared butter from the churn onto his face, Sethe interprets his act as a desperate response to his wife's bizarre deprivation of breast milk. For Sethe, the scene fills a gap in the story of her flight; it explains, in part, why Halle could not rescue her or reunite with his family. For Baby Suggs, Halle no longer exists, gone with her other seven offspring. But he is replaced by her daughter-in-law and four grandchildren, whom she welcomes with a sumptuous feast for 90, a food offering as rich as the butter that smeared Halle's face when he realized his powerlessness to stop the assault on the barn floor beneath his hiding place in the loft. These feedings symbolize a generosity denied by slavery, a hunger not soon to be alleviated, even after nationwide emancipation.

Colors are the single rays of hope that brighten Baby Suggs's last days. She particularly craves lavender and the orange squares that lessen the forbidding neutrality of the keeping room both for her and for its subsequent inhabitant, Beloved, who also gravitates toward a rich, fiery hue. Touches of red signify Beloved—she is bathed in red blood, gravitating toward a flitting cardinal, and wrenching open the cloistered red heart within Paul D. The black community, designated as Bluestone Road, is like a sapphire, a jewel that forms in nature. Like a pearl evolving around grit or a diamond forced into sparkling life from dispirited carbon, Bluestone (a way station) colors black freedom with a reassuring luster.

Metal images appear, such as the knife that Paul D grips like a harpoon as he skewers Beloved with personal questions about where she came from and where she is headed. The iron in Sethe's eyes and the iron bit in Paul D's mouth that stops him from talking with Halle about his trauma represent the dichotomy of female strength versus male impotence. The cruelties of Sweet Home stiffen Sethe against all buffetings, even loss of respect for her much-loved husband; these same indignities harness Paul D like a dray animal and stop his mouth from communicating his loss of manhood.

Without imagery, *Beloved* would be a sterile ghost story, fit only for titillating audiences into a shiver and nervous giggle. Details, richly evocative and endlessly interconnected, support the framework of *Beloved*'s plot. The multiple levels of communication perform multiple tasks:

- They tell the story.

- They describe the historic underpinnings of slavery.

- They reveal the dehumanizing effect of bondage and torture.

- They investigate the difference between male and female responses to powerlessness.

- They delineate the necessity for self-love.

- They crown the story with its ritualistic laying on of hands, the healing touch that restores wholeness.

Style

Morrison's evocative blend of detail, memory, and lyrical commentary forms a liquid stream that carries the reader along, sometimes blind or only half-aware of a significance or nuance but always attuned to the sad-expectant outlook of the channeling voice. The mesmerizing skill with which Morrison spins her tale lures the reader along with nuggets of fact—a date, an event, a motive—until the story jells in spite of the veiled meanings of the speaker's truths, half-truths, and suppositions.

The precise detail of Morrison's fiction has the ring of truth, as though she were recalling some oddment from an evening's story session long past in her childhood. For example, she explains that Sixo marks Patsy in order to deceive her master; he "punctured her calf to simulate snakebite so she could use it in some way as an excuse for not being on time to shake worms from tobacco leaves."

Women in *Beloved*

For Morrison's women, sexuality is the reward and burden of their gender. She describes Paul D's effect on females this way:

Strong women and wise saw him and told him things they only told each other: that way past the Change of Life, desire in them had suddenly become enormous, greedy, more savage than when they were fifteen, and that it embarrassed them and made them sad; that secretly they longed to die—to be quit of it—that sleep was more precious to them than any waking day.

For Morrison's post-slave era women, menopause is the resurgence of desire, a fleshly encumbrance that precedes death, a well-deserved respite from indiscriminate breeding, unsatisfactory mates, and children sold before mothers could return home to wave goodbye.

Ma'am, the elusive role model whom Sethe never fully knew, is excluded from this life cycle of virginity, puberty, loss of virginity, childbearing, menopause, and death. The artificiality of the slave lifestyle bears with it the power to lop off a life at any stage, a situation shared with men who hang from the pretty trees of Sweet Home.

For women, the suffering of procreation is compounded by seeing offspring forced into the slave milieu and by knowing that children will have no choice but to go on producing more of their kind to stock the limitless slave rolls that power the plantation system.

The bittersweet love between Sethe and her lost little girl forms the crux, the burden that overloads the scarred back, already laden with its metaphoric chokecherry tree. Sethe, the equivalent of Homer's amazon, remains in control in most situations—enough to stun Here Boy, set his broken legs, and force his eye back into the socket. The likelihood that any female could survive sexual abuse, lashing, thirst, hunger, and childbirth, yet continue to form milk in her breasts, defies scientific evidence. The fact that Sethe accomplishes all this and more is Morrison's tribute to her determination. Obsessed by the chokecherry tree, Sethe refuses to vacate the house that enslaves her to the nightmare of her dead infant. She wrestles the embodiment of her guilt to a truce so strong, so enduring that a second buggy in the yard resurrects the image of deadly spite that thwarted schoolteacher 18 years earlier.

It is fitting that a woman strong enough to crawl through woods so that she could give birth in a canoe would spawn a girl as resolute and resourceful as Denver. Although Denver is more inward and more manipulative than her confrontational mother, she recognizes the moment when

Sethe is no longer mistress of the house, when the next generation must venture down the plank road to pursue food, solace, and steady work. Even more determined than Denver is Beloved, the whirlwind force that belabors a household for 18 years, exiles two strong brothers, and edges her forthright mother to the brink of madness. Such a threesome does honor to Baby Suggs, the matriarch, whose love sheltered an entire black neighborhood and whose memory comforts and sustains them all.

A Note on Slavery

Set on the bloody side of the Ohio River, life at Sweet Home mocks the "Old Kentucky Home" of Stephen Foster's saccharine, sentimental set pieces. For Mr. Garner's male slaves, life is bondage, longing, and potential death if they step outside the prescribed norms of behavior. Baby Suggs and Sethe, separated by color, class, and privilege from Mrs. Garner, know the eternal ache of seeing their loved ones "run off . . . hanged . . . rented out, loaned out, bought up, brought back, stored up, mortgaged, won, stolen or seized." For Sethe, blessed with six years of marriage to a loving man, the only tempering mechanism for daily drudgery lies in sprigs of myrtle, salsify, and mint that sweeten the bitterness of servitude. But for Baby Suggs, too lost in a milieu of passing mates and disappearing family, reality is a slave's truth: ". . . nobody stopped playing checkers just because the pieces included her children."

For Cincinnati blacks, slavery's legacy lies beyond the whip, far from the auction block, a generation away from dogs, slave catchers, patrollers, rapists, child-sellers, iron bits, and pronged necklaces. The curse of bondage lies in the spirit that has been so dirtied that it can no longer love itself. Morrison composes her novel to honor the survivors—station keepers like Baby Suggs who have the courage and determination to fight not only the emerging Ku Klux Klan and other forms of white spite, but to wash away the baptism of silt that coats the psyche and blocks out the light. The holy Baby Suggs names the individual parts of the body that each freed slave must rescue—hands, feet, neck, liver—and concludes her sermon with an appropriate benediction: "More than your life-holding womb and your life-giving private parts, hear me now, love your heart. For this is the prize."

Beloved, the Film

Released in 1998, the film version of *Beloved* received mixed critical reviews. Those who had read the book generally appreciated the film more than those who hadn't. Anyone who has read the book can understand the challenge involved in translating Morrison's multi-layered story onto the screen. How does one handle the fluid narrative, which in the book slips effortlessly back and forth between past and present? How does one convey the atmosphere of the house or the internal lives of the various characters?

While the film addresses these issues, its success at reproducing the style, mood, and characters of the book is uneven. At points, the filmmakers capture Morrison's vision perfectly; at other times, important concepts are lost and the flow of the story becomes confused. For instance, the film beautifully depicts Baby Suggs's revival meetings in which she calls forth the children, the men, and the women. Beah Richards is spectacular as Baby, radiating the love and power on screen that you feel in the pages of the book. The scene in which the people gather, the children laugh, the men dance, and the women weep is potent in its activity and noise, and it conveys the importance of healing, community, and love even better than the book does.

On the other hand, the movie passes over some important character points, causing the narrative to possibly become confusing for those who have not read the book. For example, very little is revealed about Paul D's past or about his idea that all of his bad memories are locked in a tin where his heart should be. As a result, Paul D is a less complex character than he is in the book. Additionally, when Beloved seduces him and he calls out "Red heart, red heart!", without having a context for "red heart," the viewer is left wondering what he is talking about and perhaps sees his coupling with Beloved as a weakness rather than something he could not control.

Even with rough spots such as that one, however, *Beloved* as a whole remains faithful to the book. The dialogue is almost identical to that in the book, and the characters are portrayed nearly perfectly. Oprah Winfrey is Sethe, with her iron will tempered by sorrow and longing. As Paul D, Danny Glover conveys a friendly, personable man who possesses both intelligence and depth. Denver and Beloved are also well done, played by Kimberly Elise and Thandie Newton. Elise's Denver maintains the right balance of selfishness, craving love, and budding maturity, while Newton's Beloved can transform from a vacant beauty to an angry fiend and back again, giving us a sense that she is much more than a reincarnated two-year-old.

CliffsNotes Review

Use this CliffsNotes Review to test your understanding of the original text and to reinforce what you've learned in this book. After you work through the quotation identifications, discussion questions, and practice projects, you're well on your way to understanding a comprehensive and meaningful interpretation of Morrison's *Beloved*.

Q & A

1. Why does Sethe have the word "Beloved" carved into her daughter's headstone?

2. How does Baby Suggs get her freedom?

3. What happens to when she finds out that her mother murdered her sister?

4. What did Mrs. Garner give Sethe for a wedding present?

5. What does Beloved have on her neck?

6. What are the two columns that the schoolteacher tells his pupils to write characteristics of the slaves in?

7. Why does Sixo call out "Seven-O" as he is dying?

8. Where does Paul D first stay when he escapes from the slave labor camp?

9. Who does Denver first go to for help when Sethe, Beloved, and herself are starving?

10. Who are the "men without skin" that Beloved talks about?

Answers: (1) It is a word she remembers from her daughter's funeral service, when the minister spoke to the "Dearly Beloved." (2) Halle hires himself out from Sweet Home on Sundays for years in order to buy her freedom. (3) She goes deaf for two years. (4) Crystal earrings. (5) A scar from where Sethe cut her throat with a handsaw. (6) "Human" and "animal." (7) Thirty-Mile Woman is pregnant with Sixo's child. (8) In a Cherokee camp. (9) Lady Jones, her former teacher. (10). White men; slave owners.

Identify the Quote

Identify the speakers and the circumstances of the following quotations.

1. Velvet is like the world was just born. Clean and new and so smooth.

2. I took and put my babies where they'd be safe.

3. You got two feet, Sethe, not four.

4. What I have to do is get in my bed and lay down. I want to fix on something harmless in this world.

5. Her face is my own and I want to be there in the place where her face is and to be looking at it too.

Answers: (1) Amy Denver says this to Sethe while she is tending to the runaway slave and thinking of her own escape from servitude. (2) Sethe says this to defend her extreme actions, which were intended to prevent her children from suffering through lives of slavery. (3) Paul D makes this remark to Sethe after learning the truth about Beloved's murder and immediately before he leaves 124. (4) Baby Suggs explains why she disconnects from the black community, which turned its back on her family in its time of greatest need. (5) Beloved indicates her longing to be connected to Sethe.

Essay Questions

1. Describe the relationships that slave mothers have with their children in *Beloved*. How are these relationships affected by slavery? How are they affected by freedom?

2. What are some examples of healing in Beloved? How are people healed physically? Spiritually?

3. Discuss the use of nature imagery in *Beloved* and how it corresponds to the characters' moods or situations.

4. Describe the different ways in which white people treat African-Americans in *Beloved*. How do the African-Americans respond to such treatment?

5. How does Sethe justify her murder of Beloved? How are her actions viewed by the townspeople? By Paul D?

Practice Projects

1. Sethe's story is based on an actual slave mother, Margaret Garner, who killed her child rather than see it returned to slavery. Research Margaret Garner's story and write a report describing the similarities and differences between it and *Beloved*.

2. Create a timeline documenting the events that occur in *Beloved*.

3. Construct a Web site that other students reading *Beloved* could use. The Web site should include a page about major themes in the book, a page about Toni Morrison, and a page about slavery in the United States.

CliffsNotes Resource Center

The learning doesn't need to stop here. CliffsNotes Resource Center shows you the best of the best—links to the best information in print and online about Toni Morrison and works written by and about her. And don't think that this is all we've prepared for you; we've put all kinds of pertinent information at www.cliffsnotes.com. Look for all the terrific resources at your favorite bookstore or local library and on the Internet. When you're online, make your first stop www.cliffsnotes.com, where you'll find more useful information about *Beloved*.

Books

This CliffsNotes book provides a meaningful interpretation of Morrison's *Beloved*. If you are looking for additional information about the author and/or related works, check out these other publications:

ANDREWS, WILLIAM L. and NELLIE Y. MCKAY, eds. *Toni Morrison's Beloved: A Casebook.* Andrews and McKay approach the novel in terms of its historical context, providing documents related to the Margaret Garner story that inspired the novel. They also include seven previously-published essays on the book that discuss the novel through a wide range of critical interpretations.

DAVID, RON. *Toni Morrison Explained: A Reader's Road Map to the Novels.* New York: Random House, 2000. In this general introduction to Toni Morrison and her works, David provides commentary on Morrison's books in a friendly, conversational manner, touching briefly on Morrison's life and then examining her books in terms of language and subtext.

KUBITSCHEK, MISSY DEHN. *Toni Morrison: A Critical Companion.* This very readable work studies each of Morrison's works, including her most recent books, *Beloved, Jazz,* and *Paradise.* Each book's analysis thoroughly covers the novel's plot, character development, and themes.

PLASA, CARL, ed. *Toni Morrison: Beloved (Columbia Critical Guides).* New York: Columbia UP, 1998. Includes comprehensive overviews and concise analyses of the novel. Plasa assembles excerpts from essays, reviews, and articles on *Beloved,* offering the reader easy access to important secondary writings on the novel.

TAYLOR-GUTHRIE, DANIELLE, ed. *Conversations With Toni Morrison. Jackson, MS: University Press of Mississippi, 1994.* Taylor-Guthrie has compiled a collection of 24 interviews with Toni Morrison, arranged chronologically from 1974 to 1992. The interviews reveal Morrison's creativity, her awareness of her African-American heritage, and her cultural and societal concerns.

Internet

Check out these Web resources for more information about *Beloved:*

Toni Morrison References On The Internet. www.viconet.com/~ejb/intro.htm. Contains links to Morrison's biography, a bibliography of her works and works written about her, and essays on her books, including *Beloved.*

The Nobel Prize Internet Archive: Toni Morrison. nobelprizes.com/nobel/literature/1993a.html. Includes materials relating to Morrison's books and her winning the Nobel Prize, such as her Nobel lecture and the press release announcing her receipt of the award.

Anniina's Toni Morrison Page. www.luminarium.org/contemporary/tonimorrison/toni.htm. An easy-to-navigate Web site devoted to Toni Morrison. It contains a page that focuses specifically on *Beloved* and include links to other *Beloved* sites on the Internet and essays about the novel.

Toni Morrison's Beloved: Reflections of the Past. www.cwrl.utexas.edu/~maria/morrison/toni.htm. The University of Texas's site devoted to Toni Morrison and *Beloved.* The project includes Morrison's biography and essays on history, families, rememory, and Sethe's character development.

Africans in America: America's Journey Through Slavery. www.pbs.org/wgbh/aia/. An excellent site to learn more about slavery in America. The companion site to the PBS series, this Web site examines the economic and intellectual foundations of slavery in America and the global economy that prospered from it. The site includes historical narratives, resource banks, and teachers' guides.

American Slave Narratives: An Online Anthology. `xroads.virginia.`
`edu/~HYPER/wpa/wpahome.html`. Contains more than 2,300
interviews with former slaves that were conducted from 1936 to
1938 by writers and journalists through the Works Progress Admin-
istration. The narratives provide first-hand accounts of nineteenth-
century slavery, including labor, resistance and flight, family life,
relations with masters, and religious belief.

Video

DEMME, JONATHAN, dir. *Beloved.* Touchstone Pictures, 1998. An
adaptation that remains faithful to Morrison's novel, especially in
dialogue and characterization. The haunting score and cinematog-
raphy help to convey the atmosphere and mood of the book.

Recordings

MORRISON, TONI. *Beloved.* New York: Random House Audio, 1998.
This unabridged audio version of the novel was nominated for a
Grammy for Best Spoken Word Recording. Morrison gives her characters life and depth with her rich voice and gives the reader a new
appreciation of the work.

Index

NUMBERS

124 Bluestone Road, 37, 98
   appearence of Beloved's ghost, 13
   arrival of slave catchers, 31
   Lady Jones's charity toward, 82
   Paul D's departure from, 66
   Sethe's arrival at, 45

A

Aeneas, 49
Africans in America Web site, 111
Alfred, Georgia, 30, 39, 48, 50, 64, 75
American Slave Narratives Web site, 112
Anniina's Toni Morrison Page Web site, 111
arrival
   of Beloved, 35–36
   of Paul D, 24
As I Lay Dying, 94
author awards, 9–10
author, personal background, 2–7
author degrees, 10

B

Baby Suggs
   burial of, 67
   characterization of, 15, 91
   flashback of reunion with Sethe, 59
   freedom, 107
   heart condition, 47
background of Toni Morrison, 2–7
banishment of Beloved's ghost, 24
Beloved
   arrival of, 35–36
   characterization of, 14, 89
   choking Sethe, 46
   death of, 25
   Denver's relationship with, 53
   description of death, 73
   disintegration of, 87
   exorcism from 124 Bluestone Road, 51
   gravestone, 14, 25, 107

   murder of, 61
   paradox of death, 71
   Paul D's investigation of, 39
   Paul D's relationship with, 56
   pregnancy, 80
   prevention of Paul D and Sethe's
      relationship, 51–52
   questions about Sethe's past, 37
   revelation of her past, 39
   scars on neck, 107
   as symbol of all slaves, 55
Beloved, publication of, 6
   film version, 105–106
   form of, 95
   motifs, 101–103
   settings, 98–99
   style, 103
   synopsis of, 12, 14
   themes, 100–101
   women in, 104
benediction of Beloved's death, 74
benevolent masters, 60
bestiality as motif, 25
bildungsroman, 12
Black Book, The, 5
Black Boy, 95
black community's shunning of Sethe, 47
Bluest Eye, The, 4
boat as symbol, 43
Bodwin, Edwin
   characterization of, 17
   Sethe's murder attempt of, 82–83
Bodwin, Miss, 17
books concerning Toni Morrison, 110
boxwood bushes, 30
Brandywine, Paul D's sale to, 49
breast images, 102
breastfeeding as motif, 25, 38
Breedlove, Pecola, 4
Brown, Claude, 4
Brown, Sterling, 3
Buddy, Mr., 16
Buddy, Mrs., 16
Buglar, 15, 57
burial of Baby Suggs, 67

C

career, Toni Morrison teaching, 4–7
Carmichael, Stokely, 4
carnival, 33

character descriptions, 14–17
characterization
    Baby Suggs, 91
    Beloved, 89
    Denver, 90
    Paul D, 91
    schoolteacher., 92
    Sethe, 89
Cherokee, 48, 49
childhood of Toni Morrison, 2
chronology of plot, 17–20
Church of the Holy Redeemer, 75
Cincinnati, 59
Color Purple, The, 95
colors as motif, 25, 102
coming-of-age novels, 12
conjuring of Denver's memories, 30
Cornell University, 4
critical essays about *Beloved,* 94
critical response to *Beloved,* 8

D

death
    Beloved's, 25
    Garner's, 75
    paradox of Beloved's death, 71
Denver, 72
    Beloved's relationship with, 53
    characterization of, 14, 90
    deterioration of home life, 80
    effect of sister's murder on, 107
    fear of losing Beloved, 54
    memories, conjuring, 30
    as recluse, 71
    relationship with Beloved, 42
    visit to Lady Jones, 82
    withdrawal from community, 81
Denver, Amy, 13, 15, 42–43
destructiveness of living in the past, 81
diaspora, 73
disintegration of Beloved, 87
dismemberment, images of, 57
Dreaming Emmett, 6

E

Edenic symbols, boxwood bushes, 31
editorship at Random House, 4
education, Toni Morrison, 3–7
effect of Beloved's murder on Denver, 107
Ella, 17

epic journeys, plot parallels with, 48
epigraph, 23
escape from Sweet Home, Paul D's failed
    attempt, 75
essays about *Beloved,* 94
Eurocentrism, 8
exorcism of Beloved's ghost from 124
    Bluestone Road, 51

F

family of Toni Morrison, 2
female genitalia as motif, 26
film version of *Beloved,* 105–106
flashbacks, Baby Suggs, 59
foreshadowing
    Baby Suggs's heart condition, 47
    at carnival, 33
form of novel, 95
Foster, Stephen, 60, 105
Four Horsemen of the Apocalypse, 62
freedom, Baby Suggs, 107

G

Garner, Margaret
    inspiration for *Beloved,* 7, 110
    slave narrative about, 6
Garner, Mr., 15
Garner, Mrs., 15, 71, 107
Garner, Paul A, 16
Garner, Paul D. *See* Paul D
Garner, Paul F, 16
gestalt, 30
ghost of Beloved
    description of death, 73
    banishment of, 24
    strength of, 51
gothic conventions of Beloved's ghost, 87
grace as theme, 96
Grapes of Wrath, 94
guilt of Stamp Paid, 66

H

Halle Suggs, 28, 39
    departure from Sethe, 39
    disappearance of, 40
    escape from schoolteacher, 13
    relationship with Sethe, 28
    Sethe's selection as mate, 13, 101

harmony as theme, 67
healing touch as motif, 38, 96
heart as motif, 26
Heart of Darkness, 12, 95
Here Boy, return of, 85
Hi Man, 16
historical fiction, 12
Howard, 15, 57
Howard University, 4
hubris as theme, 67
Huckleberry Finn, 95

I

ice skates as symbol, 68
idols of Toni Morrison, Maria Tallchief, 3
images
    of breasts, 102
    of female genitals, 31
    of metal, 102
    of milk, 102
    of water, 101
infanticide, 83
influence of Baby Suggs, 45–46
inspiration for *Beloved,* 12
internal monologue, Sethe, 72
Internet. *See* Web sites
introduction of motifs, 25
iron as motif, 26, 39–40, 73

J

Jane Eyre, 95
Janey Wagon, 80
Jazz, 7
Jenny Whitlow. *See* Baby Suggs
Jones, Lady, 17, 46, 82
Joshua. *See* Stamp Paid

L

Lady Jones, 17, 46, 82
Locke, Alan, 3
Lorain, Ohio, 2
Lord, Nelson, 17, 46

M

Ma'am, 16, 37, 104
manumission, 59
Mark 10:14, 46

marriage of Sethe and Halle, 28
Medea, 49
Meditations, 95
memories
    Baby Suggs, lack of, 38
    Denver, conjuring of, 30
    Paul D, of life on the road, 40
    Paul D, of prison, 48
    Sethe, 31
    Sethe, of Mrs. Garner, 71
men without skin, 74, 107
metal images, 102
metaphors, sexual encounters, 28
milk images, 102
Mister, 40, 76
Morrison, Harold, 4
Morrison, Toni
    critical response, 8
    honors, 9–10
    personal background, 2–7
motherhood, exploration of psychology, 12
motifs, 25, 101–103
    healing touch, 38, 96
    way station, 40
murder of Beloved, 61

N

Nan, 16
Native Son, 95
nature as symbol, 97
Nelson, Lord, 17, 46
nephews, schoolteacher's, 67
Nobel Prize for *Beloved,* 10
Nobel Prize Internet Archive, Toni Morrison
    Web site, 111
numerological possibilities in plot, 25

O

Odysseus, 49
oral traditions, 9
Orpheus, 49

P

Paradise, 7
paradox of Beloved's death, 71
pathetic fallacy, 43
Patsy. *See* The Thirty-Mile Woman

Paul D, 15
  arrival of, 24
  Beloved's relationship with, 56
  capture of, 39
  characterization of, 64, 91
  confrontation of truth about Beloved's
    death, 63–64
  decision to stay with Sethe, 33
  effect of slavery on, 76
  escape from prison, 107
  investigation of Beloved, 39
  memories of life on the road, 40
  prison, memories of, 48
  recalling Garner's death, 75
  reconciliation with Sethe, 56
  Sethe's relationship with, 51–52
  sexual encounter with Sethe, 28
  Stamp Paid's atonement, 78
  Stamp Paid's revelation about Beloved's
    death, 63–64
personal background of Toni Morrison, 2–7
Pike, Reverend, 17
plants as motif, 25
plot
  chronology of, 17–20
  development of post-slavery influence on
    Paul D, 33
  numerological possibilities in, 25
pregnancy, Beloved, 80
prison
  Paul D's memories of, 40, 48
  Sethe's term for Beloved's murder, 83
psychology of motherhood, 12
publication of *Beloved*, 6
Pulitzer Prize for *Beloved*, 10

R

Ragtime, 95
Random House, 4
reconciliation of Paul D and Sethe, 56
recordings of Beloved, 112
red heart as symbol, 97
reincarnation of Beloved, 36
relationships
  Beloved and Paul D, 56
  Beloved and Sethe, 38
  Denver and Beloved, 42, 53
  Sethe and Paul D, 28, 51–52
religious conventions, 46

restaurant, Paul D's search for Sethe, 56
resurrection as motif, 26
return of Here Boy, 85
revelation of Beloved's past, 39
Reverend Pike, 17
Romans 9, 23

S

sale to Brandywine of Paul D, 49
Sawyer, 17, 56
Scarlet Letter, The, 94
scars on Beloved's neck, 107
schoolteacher, 13, 62, 107
  capture of Paul D, 39
  characterization of, 16, 92
  nephews, 18–20
Sethe
  arrival at Sweet Home, 28
  Beloved's questions about her past, 37
  betrayed by Stamp Paid, 66
  black community's shunning of, 47
  characterization of, 14, 89
  choked by Beloved, 46
  confrontation of truth about Beloved's
    death, 63–64
  effect of slavery on, 76
  influence of Baby Suggs, 45–46
  memories, 31
  memories of Mrs. Garner, 71
  murder attempt of Edwin Bodwin,
    82–83
  Paul D's relationship with, 51–52
  protection of Denver, 30
  reconciliation with Paul D, 56
  release from prison, 14
  sexual encounter with Paul D, 28
settings of novel, 98–99
Seven-O, 107
sexual encounters
  metaphor, 28
  Paul D and Sethe, 28, 58
sexuality of women in *Beloved*, 104
Sixo, 16, 56, 107
slavery, 105
  effect on Paul D and Sethe, 76
  inspiration for novel, 12
  victimization of former slaves, 67
Song of Solomon, 6
Sophie's Choice, 94

Sound and the Fury, The, 94
Stamp Paid, 45, 62
   atonement for interfering with Paul D
     and Sethe, 78
   characterization of, 15
   effect of slavery on, 78
   guilt of revelation to Paul D, 66
   revelation to Paul D about Beloved's
     death, 63–64
strength of Beloved's ghost, 51
style of Morrison's writing, 103
Suggs, Baby
   burial of, 67
   characterization of, 15, 91
   flashback, 59
   freedom, 107
   influence of, 45–46
   lack of memories, 38
Suggs, Halle. *See* Halle Suggs
Sula, 5
superstition
   arrival of Beloved, 35
   as motif, 26
Sweet Home, 98
   celebration of Sethe and Halle's
     honeymoon, 28
   Paul D's memories of, 40
   Sethe's arrival at, 13, 25, 28
   Sethe's departure from, 24
symbols
   boat, 43
   boxwood bushes, 31
   Christ's crown, 62
   dismemberment, 57
   Four Horsemen of the Apocalypse, 62
   hummingbirds, 64
   ice skates, 68
   nature, 97
   red heart, 97
   water, 85
synopsis, 12, 14

T

Tallchief, Maria, 3
Tar Baby, 6
teaching career of Toni Morrison, 4–7
Texas Southern University, 4
themes, 100, 101
   grace, 96
   harmony, 67

hubris, 67
motifs, 25
Thirty-Mile Woman, The, 16
Toni Morrison On The Internet
   Web site, 111
Toni Morrison's Beloved, Reflections of the Past
   Web site, 111
Turn of the Screw, 94

U

Ulysses, 94
Underground Railroad, 17

V

Vashti, 15
victimization of former slaves, 67
video, *Beloved,* 112

W

Wagon, Janey, 17
water,
   images of, 101
   as symbol, 85
way station as motif, 40
Web sites
   Africans in America, 111
   American Slave Narratives, 112
   Anniina's Toni Morrison Page, 111
   Nobel Prize Internet Archive, Toni
     Morrison, 111
   Toni Morrison On The Internet, 111
   Toni Morrison's Beloved, Reflections of the
     Past, 111
Whitlow, 16
withdrawal of Denver from community, 81
Wofford, George, 2
Wofford, Ramah Willis, 2
women in *Beloved,* 104
writing career of Toni Morrison, 4–7
Wuthering Heights, 95

NOTES

Personal Background

An unflinching champion of her race and its heritage, Toni Morrison confesses to "[thinking] the unthinkable." In her Pulitzer Prize-winning novel *Beloved,* she explores infanticide, rape, seduction, madness, passion, wisdom, alienation, powerlessness, regret, tyranny, and the supernatural. A bold novelist, she has staked out fictional turf on which to dramatize the fact that black people, the center of her microcosms, are not marginal racial anomalies, but a genuine human society. In rebuttal of less inclusive philosophies, Morrison states: "There is a notion out in the land that there are black people or Indians or some other marginal group, and if you write about the world from that point of view, somehow it is considered lesser." Rejecting anything other than full membership in humanity for black people, she asserts her credo: "We are people, not aliens. We live, we love, and we die."

Childhood

Although reared in the North, Toni Morrison is the genetic and historical offspring of southern traditions. These traditions derive from her maternal grandfather, a carpenter and farmer who, seeing no chance for advancement in Kentucky's racism and poverty, moved his family to Ohio. Morrison's father, sharecropper George Wofford, had similar reasons to escape racial oppression in Georgia and relocate in northern shipyards, where he found welding jobs that he supplemented by washing cars. In the relative calm of the far north, Wofford, an embittered racist, still found reasons to distrust "every word and every gesture of every white man on earth." In contrast, Morrison's mother, Ramah Willis Wofford, a more educated, trusting person than her husband, offered her family a gentler, less vitriolic point of view concerning race relations.

The second of the four Wofford children, Morrison (née Chloe Anthony Wofford) was born February 18, 1931, and grew up on the western fringe of Cleveland, which sits on the south shore of Lake Erie. In the multicultural environment of Lorain, Ohio—a steel town of around 75,000, blending Czech, German, Irish, Greek, Italian, Serb, Mexican, and black suburbanites—Morrison experienced exclusion but did not suffer the intense racism leveled at other black writers, as demonstrated in the autobiographies of Maya Angelou, Dick Gregory, and Richard Wright. Although a landlord torched their apartment with the Woffords inside in 1933, Ramah, in order to foster mental health,

LIFE AND BACKGROUND OF THE AUTHOR

Personal Background 2

Teaching and Writing 4

Critical Response 8

Honors 9

How to Use This Book

CliffsNotes Morrison's *Beloved* supplements the original work, giving you background information about Toni Morrison, an introduction to the novel, a graphical character map, critical commentaries, expanded glossaries, and a comprehensive index. CliffsNotes Review tests your comprehension of the original text and reinforces learning with questions and answers, practice projects, and more. For further information on Toni Morrison and *Beloved,* check out the CliffsNotes Resource Center.

CliffsNotes provides the following icons to highlight essential elements of particular interest:

Reveals the underlying themes in the work.

Helps you to more easily relate to or discover the depth of a character.

Uncovers elements such as setting, atmosphere, mystery, passion, violence, irony, symbolism, tragedy, foreshadowing, and satire.

Enables you to appreciate the nuances of words and phrases.

Don't Miss Our Web Site

Discover classic literature as well as modern-day treasures by visiting the CliffsNotes Web site at www.cliffsnotes.com. You can obtain a quick download of a CliffsNotes title, purchase a title in print form, browse our catalog, or view online samples.

You'll also find interactive tools that are fun and informative, links to interesting Web sites, tips, articles, and additional resources to help you, not only for literature, but for test prep, finance, careers, computers, and the Internet too. See you at www.cliffsnotes.com!

Chapter 25 78
    Summary 78
    Commentary 78
    Glossary 79
Chapter 26 80
    Summary 80
    Commentary 81
    Glossary 83
Chapter 27 85
    Summary 85
    Commentary 85
    Glossary 86
Chapter 28 87
    Summary 87
    Commentary 87

Character Analyses 88
    Sethe 89
    Beloved 89
    Denver 90
    Baby Suggs 91
    Paul D 91
    schoolteacher 92

Critical Essays 93
    Beloved and Its Forerunners 94
    Form 95
    Settings 98
    Themes 100
    Motifs 101
    Style 103
    Women in Beloved 104
    A Note on Slavery 105
    Beloved, the Film 105

CliffsNotes Review 107
    Q&A 107
    Identify the Quote 108
    Essay Questions 108
    Practice Projects 109

CliffsNotes Resource Center 110
    Books 110
    Internet 111
    Video 112
    Recordings 112

Index 113

CliffsNotes™

The Odyssey
Oedipus Trilogy
Of Human Bondage
Of Mice and Men
The Old Man and
the Sea
Old Testament
Oliver Twist
The Once and
Future King
One Day in the Life of
Ivan Denisovich
One Flew Over the
Cuckoo's Nest
100 Years of Solitude
O'Neill's Plays
Othello
Our Town
The Outsiders
The Ox Bow Incident
Paradise Lost
A Passage to India
The Pearl
The Pickwick Papers
The Picture of
Dorian Gray
Pilgrim's Progress
The Plague
Plato's Euthyphro…
Plato's The Republic
Poe's Short Stories
A Portrait of the
Artist…
The Portrait of a Lady
The Power and
the Glory
Pride and Prejudice
The Prince
The Prince and
the Pauper
A Raisin in the Sun
The Red Badge of
Courage
The Red Pony
The Return of the
Native
Richard II
Richard III

The Rise of
Silas Lapham
Robinson Crusoe
Roman Classics
Romeo and Juliet
The Scarlet Letter
A Separate Peace
Shakespeare's
Comedies
Shakespeare's Histories
Shakespeare's
Minor Plays
Shakespeare's Sonnets
Shakespeare's Tragedies
Shaw's Pygmalion &
Arms…
Silas Marner
Sir Gawain…Green
Knight
Sister Carrie
Slaughterhouse-five
Snow Falling on Cedars
Song of Solomon
Sons and Lovers
The Sound and the Fury
Steppenwolf &
Siddhartha
The Stranger
The Sun Also Rises
T.S. Eliot's Poems &
Plays
A Tale of Two Cities
The Taming of the
Shrew
Tartuffe, Misanthrope…
The Tempest
Tender Is the Night
Tess of the D'Urbervilles
Their Eyes Were
Watching God
Things Fall Apart
The Three Musketeers
To Kill a Mockingbird
Tom Jones
Tom Sawyer
Treasure Island &
Kidnapped
The Trial

Tristram Shandy
Troilus and Cressida
Twelfth Night
Ulysses
Uncle Tom's Cabin
The Unvanquished
Utopia
Vanity Fair
Vonnegut's Works
Waiting for Godot
Walden
Walden Two
War and Peace
Who's Afraid of
Virginia…
Winesburg, Ohio
The Winter's Tale
The Woman Warrior
Worldly Philosophers
Wuthering Heights
A Yellow Raft in
Blue Water

Check Out the All-New CliffsNotes Guides

TECHNOLOGY TOPICS
Balancing Your Check-
book with Quicken
Buying and Selling
on eBay™
Buying Your First PC
Creating a Winning
PowerPoint 2000
Presentation
Creating Web Pages
with HTML
Creating Your First
Web Page
Exploring the World
with Yahoo!
Getting on the Internet
Going Online with AOL
Making Windows 98
Work for You

Setting Up a
Windows 98
Home Network
Shopping Online Safely
Upgrading and
Repairing Your PC
Using Your First iMac™
Using Your First PC
Writing Your First
Computer Program

PERSONAL FINANCE TOPICS
Budgeting & Saving
Your Money
Getting a Loan
Getting Out of Debt
Investing for the
First Time
Investing in
401(k) Plans
Investing in IRAs
Investing in
Mutual Funds
Investing in the
Stock Market
Managing Your Money
Planning Your
Retirement
Understanding
Health Insurance
Understanding
Life Insurance

CAREER TOPICS
Delivering a Winning
Job Interview
Finding a Job
on the Web
Getting a Job
Writing a Great Resume

@ cliffsnotes.com

CliffsNotes

LITERATURE NOTES

Absalom, Absalom!
The Aeneid
Agamemnon
Alice in Wonderland
All the King's Men
All the Pretty Horses
All Quiet on the
   Western Front
All's Well &
   Merry Wives
American Poets of the
   20th Century
American Tragedy
Animal Farm
Anna Karenina
Anthem
Antony and Cleopatra
Aristotle's Ethics
As I Lay Dying
The Assistant
As You Like It
Atlas Shrugged
Autobiography of
   Ben Franklin
Autobiography of
   Malcolm X
The Awakening
Babbit
Bartleby & Benito
   Cereno
The Bean Trees
The Bear
The Bell Jar
Beloved
Beowulf
The Bible
Billy Budd & Typee
Black Boy
Black Like Me
Bleak House
Bless Me, Ultima
The Bluest Eye & Sula
Brave New World
Brothers Karamazov

The Call of the Wild &
   White Fang
Candide
The Canterbury Tales
Catch-22
Catcher in the Rye
The Chosen
The Color Purple
Comedy of Errors...
Connecticut Yankee
The Contender
The Count of
   Monte Cristo
Crime and Punishment
The Crucible
Cry, the Beloved
   Country
Cyrano de Bergerac
Daisy Miller &
   Turn...Screw
David Copperfield
Death of a Salesman
The Deerslayer
Diary of Anne Frank
Divine Comedy-I.
   Inferno
Divine Comedy-II.
   Purgatorio
Divine Comedy-III.
   Paradiso
Doctor Faustus
Dr. Jekyll and Mr. Hyde
Don Juan
Don Quixote
Dracula
Electra & Medea
Emerson's Essays
Emily Dickinson Poems
Emma
Ethan Frome
The Faerie Queene
Fahrenheit 451
Far from the Madding
   Crowd
A Farewell to Arms
Farewell to Manzanar
Fathers and Sons
Faulkner's Short Stories

Faust Pt. I & Pt. II
The Federalist
Flowers for Algernon
For Whom the Bell Tolls
The Fountainhead
Frankenstein
The French
   Lieutenant's Woman
The Giver
Glass Menagerie &
   Streetcar
Go Down, Moses
The Good Earth
The Grapes of Wrath
Great Expectations
The Great Gatsby
Greek Classics
Gulliver's Travels
Hamlet
The Handmaid's Tale
Hard Times
Heart of Darkness &
   Secret Sharer
Hemingway's
   Short Stories
Henry IV Part 1
Henry IV Part 2
Henry V
House Made of Dawn
The House of the
   Seven Gables
Huckleberry Finn
I Know Why the
   Caged Bird Sings
Ibsen's Plays I
Ibsen's Plays II
The Idiot
Idylls of the King
The Iliad
Incidents in the Life of
   a Slave Girl
Inherit the Wind
Invisible Man
Ivanhoe
Jane Eyre
Joseph Andrews
The Joy Luck Club
Jude the Obscure

Julius Caesar
The Jungle
Kafka's Short Stories
Keats & Shelley
The Killer Angels
King Lear
The Kitchen God's Wife
The Last of the
   Mohicans
Le Morte d'Arthur
Leaves of Grass
Les Miserables
A Lesson Before Dying
Light in August
The Light in the Forest
Lord Jim
Lord of the Flies
The Lord of the Rings
Lost Horizon
Lysistrata & Other
   Comedies
Macbeth
Madame Bovary
Main Street
The Mayor of
   Casterbridge
Measure for Measure
The Merchant
   of Venice
Middlemarch
A Midsummer Night's
   Dream
The Mill on the Floss
Moby-Dick
Moll Flanders
Mrs. Dalloway
Much Ado About
   Nothing
My Ántonia
Mythology
Narr. ...Frederick
   Douglass
Native Son
New Testament
Night
1984
Notes from the
   Underground

NOTES

NOTES